A fresh approach

Productivity
Management

___

A fresh approach

John Heap
Immediate Past Chairman, Institute of Management Services
Head of Computing Services, Leeds Polytechnic

CASSELL

Cassell Educational Limited
Villiers House, 41/47 Strand, London WC2N 5JE, England
387 Park Avenue South, New York, NY 10016–8810, USA

First published 1992

British Library Cataloguing in Publication Data
A catalogue record for this book is available from the British Library

ISBN 0–304–32556–2
    0–304–32307–1 pbk

Library of Congress Cataloging-in-Publication Data
Heap, John, 1946–
    Productivity management: a fresh approach/John Heap.
        p.   cm.
    Includes index.
    ISBN 0–304–32556–2 (hardback) – ISBN 0–304–32307–1
(paperback)
    1. Industrial productivity – Management.   I. Title.
HD56.H43   1992
658.3'14 – dc20   91–33366
                                                        CIP

Typeset by Fakenham Photosetting Limited, Fakenham, Norfolk
Printed and bound in Great Britain by Dotesios Ltd., Trowbridge, Wiltshire

Contents

Preface

Productivity is important. Improving productivity is the only sure way of increasing the size of the cake we all want to share. Yet the debate on productivity and productivity improvement seems to have run out of steam and 'quality' has become the new watchword. Part One of this book re-examines and widens the concept of productivity and relates it to such issues as quality and customer service. It introduces the term 'top-line productivity' to represent this wider and much more useful view of what we should mean when we use the term productivity. Part Two demonstrates that performance and top-line productivity in particular can be measured – an important part of the management process. Part Three looks at productivity improvement from the potential for productivity. Part Four looks at specific productivity improvement approaches and techniques. Finally, Part Five introduces the top-line productivity improvement programme, through which productivity improvement can be addressed on a continual basis by and throughout the whole organisation.

The book is aimed at a wide audience. It moves from a conceptual framework to detailed action plans. It is aimed at business and management students who want to explore the nature of productivity and relate productivity improvement to alternative business strategies. Each chapter finishes with a set of keynotes to emphasise the main points of the chapter and provide a revision aid or executive summary. The book is also suitable for, and appropriate to, practising managers who want to improve productivity within their own organisations.

PART ONE

Why productivity?

Introduction

The concept of productivity is vaguely understood by many people and poorly addressed by most organisations. The first section of this book attempts to show the true meaning and importance of productivity, and introduces a new concept: that of 'top-line productivity'. Top-line productivity is an attempt to move away from the narrow view of productivity held by most organisations and to increase awareness of the importance of productivity improvement to the future wellbeing of all organisations. It allows organisations to attack productivity on a much broader front and to use productivity improvement as a means of co-ordinating overall review of organisational activity.

Productivity improvement must take place in an era of rapid change; this section also introduces some of the environmental variables that make a productivity review essential for an organisation. Change necessitates change; if the environment is subject to change, the organisation must respond by making appropriate changes in its own structures, policies and procedures. Failure to respond, and to anticipate change, means that opportunities are lost and problems are created.

Productivity is the key determinant of value and is closely related to all the other factors that influence value: quality, service, price and so on. Any discussion of productivity must be broad enough to include all of these factors and address the issues that arise from an attempt to undertake an integrated approach to improving organisational effectiveness and wellbeing.

The aim of this part of the book is to provide the necessary background to an understanding of the importance of productivity. This is needed before we can start to construct a productivity improvement programme for an organisation that ensures that the quality and service revolution can take place, but one that can take place secure in the knowledge that it is controlled and co-ordinated as part of a wider process of organisational improvement. The remaining parts of the book will take us through an examination of the concepts of productivity measurement and then into how we can establish such a broad, all-encompassing productivity improvement programme.

1 What is productivity and how does it relate to quality?

Duality of aim

The 'quality revolution' has attracted much media attention over the last few years and has persuaded large numbers of organisations to undergo quality accreditation and to undertake quality programmes, customer care programmes, service audits and so on. Quality improvement has, at least nominally, replaced productivity improvement as the prime aim of organisations. Yet, when figures on industrial performance are quoted on a national and international basis, it is still productivity that is used as the comparator of, say, the 'strength' of UK industry in relation to its competitors. Why has this duality of aim emerged – with productivity being the measure of national wellbeing and quality being the measure of organisational wellbeing? Is there a link between the two?

The term 'productivity' has been in usage for many years, yet it is often abused and poorly understood by many who use it. The term has gone through periods when it was a fashionable term discussed at all levels of society (and included in the legislative process of the nation), and through periods when it was considered a term not to be used in polite society and was relegated to a murky background.

Most people when faced with the term have some understanding of its use but would be hard-pressed to offer a definition. The dictionary is not much help since it simply defines productivity as 'the quality or state of being productive'. This definition gives rise to two problems. Firstly, it leads to the common problem that productivity is often confused with production; organisations that increase their output often make claims about productivity increases which may not stand up to scrutiny. Secondly, the definition, although undoubtedly true, is too vague a concept to be of much use to industrial or commercial organisations as a means of analysing or improving their 'state of being productive'. Yet surely this is an important aim.

The traditional approach to clarifying the meaning has been to avoid formulating a definition in words but instead to represent it as a simple ratio:

Productivity is the ratio of output to input[1]

This can be more easily explained by the following. If the organisation (whatever type and whichever sector it is in) is seen as being a simple resource conversion system of the form:

3

Resource inputs —— Organisation —— Goods/services

then

$$\text{Productivity} = \frac{\text{Output}}{\text{Input}} = \frac{\text{Value of goods/services}}{\text{Cost of resources consumed}}$$

This is deceptively simple. Again, if we need to make practical use of the term, we need to go on and ask such questions as:

- Which resources?

- How are these measured?

- How do we determine value?

- Is the timescale of measurement important?

and suddenly, a simple ratio becomes much more complex.

Perhaps if most people have some understanding of the term, we should ask whether a definition is important. That largely depends on whether we consider the pursuit of improved productivity itself to be important.

Measuring productivity
Productivity is discussed and measured at a number of levels starting with the international and national and moving down to measurement by industrial sector, then at organisational level and finally at suborganisational levels, perhaps down to the level of individuals. Interest in productivity measures at a national level, for the economy or for particular sectors of it, is important in that productivity improvement is seen as the only valid way to pay for increased standards of living. Increased productivity can thus be used by a government as a measure of the success of its economic policies in so far as they promote, assist and support productivity improvement in individual organisations. Governments of all countries, of all political hues, are searching for economic growth – ideally, growth of a higher rate than their main competitors. Economic growth is dependent on productivity growth. The standard of living of a community is generally increased by increasing the amount of goods and services produced. We all want to improve our lot by having more labour-saving devices in our home, by having more and better holidays, more leisure time and things to do in it, and so on. This can be achieved in two ways: by increasing the number of people in employment to provide the additional goods and services, or by increasing the productivity of the organisations in which they work. Productivity growth increases the size of the 'cake'; otherwise, it can only be redistributed. If productivity is constant, output can only grow by using more resources; the sup-

4

pliers of these additional resources are likely to consume at least a major part of and perhaps the whole of the value of the additional output as compensation.

Productivity is most useful when used, as at the national level, as a comparator. A single measure of productivity is of little use: to measure the productivity of a car manufacturer and arrive at a measure of productivity of, say, 0.035 cars per man-hour tells us nothing about how well or how badly the organisation is performing. Only when we compare the productivity of two nations, two organisations, two departments or two groups do we get an indication of areas that are 'good' or 'bad'. Thus, if we could measure a second car manufacturer and find that productivity there (measured on the same basis) was 0.050 cars per man-hour, we start to make judgements about the relative performance of the two organisations. When undertaking such comparisons we need to compare the actual level, as measured by some appropriate index, and the rate of change of this index. If the productivity of an organisation is measured and compared with another similar organisation, and is found to be inferior, there may be cause for concern. Naturally, that concern is much greater if the rate of improvement is lower than that of the competitor – if the gap is widening.

Measures must also be treated with care since productivity is influenced by external environmental changes. In a recession, for example, productivity of organisations tends to fall – at least at first. One reason is that some employees become underutilised but may be needed to maintain an 'overhead' level of labour. The flight crew and cabin crews of an aircraft are needed whether the aircraft is flying with a full complement of passengers or not. It may be possible to reduce the number of people involved in the cabin crew in the face of a long-term downturn on air passengers but the productivity, as measured by passenger flying miles per man-hour would certainly be lowered. (This raises the problem of what are effective productivity measures – an issue we pursue in a later chapter.) There is also a gap between a recession starting – if we could identify such a point in time – and its starting to bite. Management teams are understandably reluctant to start laying off employees since they realise that by doing so they are discarding valuable assets (trained employees) which might be difficult to replace when the recession ends.

The productivity of nations often, also, measures the productivity of those organisations that are producing. Yet, in national terms, those people who are unemployed are a resource that is not being utilised at all – and is consuming resources. Thus, if we were to measure the output, in terms of gross domestic product (GDP) for example, and divide it by all available resources, we would get a considerably worse figure than if we measure the productivity of employed people. The productivity of such organisations may rise, but the overall productivity of the nation may simultaneously fall.

Relative productivity levels can be important to the growing number of companies that operate on a global basis; and it is now becoming common for such companies to specialise parts of their operation on specific sites, in specific countries. Our car manufacturer may well make his engines in Spain, his gearboxes in France, bodyshells in the UK and carry out final assembly in Germany. Comparisons of productivity between nations are increasingly being used as part of the decision-making process by such global organisations to help decide where to site a new manufacturing plant or distribution centre. Similarly, comparisons are used by governments and development agencies to attempt to attract new manufacturing plants from such global organisations.

Productivity is thus the only secure way of improving a nation's balance of payments, of controlling inflation and of providing more leisure time. The reference to leisure time is important in that it shows that improved productivity can be linked both to higher standards of living and improved quality of life – an increasingly common aim of both nations and individuals.

We seem only recently to have recognised the fact that the world's natural resources are limited while the range of man's desires and wants shows signs of being limitless. If these resources are to be conserved, to maintain prosperity into the future, then material and energy productivity must be increased.

When we talk of natural resources, we are normally referring to minerals, fossil fuels and so on. The greatest of the 'natural resources' is the human one – people. Although globally the population is still growing, in specific areas it is in decline. In much of the Western world, for example, the number of young people becoming available for work is predicted to drop significantly over the next few years. This phenomenon has become known as the 'demographic timebomb'. It has a number of implications: one is that it is going to become harder for employing organisations to attract employees and to retain existing ones. It is anticipated that, in the UK, employing organisations will in the future pay much more attention to the recruit-ment of mature female 'returners'. The other implication is that organisations are going to have to operate with fewer people. In either case, the payments made to these employees (including the benefits that may be used to attract them – for example, child-care facilities to attract women with children of preschool age) are likely to rise. In this case labour productivity must rise if the same 'value' of output is to be produced. Since productivity is a composite entity, this can be achieved by raising the value contributed by one of the other resource classes (e.g. by more capital investment) or by actually making the workforce more productive. Thus the pressure for increased productivity is going to become greater in the future, and productivity must be addressed as a multifactor, inter-related issue.

Since productivity is both a national and an organisational issue, it must be attacked on both fronts. Governments have a part to play by establishing conditions which are favourable to and encourage organisations to raise their productivity levels. This may include the economic development strategy of the nation (or spe-cially designated areas within it), the taxation system, and the employment legis-lation and policies.

At the organisational level, the traditional means of attacking productivity has been through addressing changes in working methods, largely in a mechanical way. Techniques such as work study and organisation and methods (O&M) are used to *quantity vs quality*

examine ways of working, and to bring about changes that typically result in lower costs, either through reducing the number of people involved in a given task, by reducing the variety of components manufactured, or by some other method of cost reduction. The analysis of incurred costs is an important but – as we shall see – not the only aspect of productivity improvement.

Nowadays at the organisational level, we have suggested that the current 'fashion' is for drives to improve quality. However, such a drive may well increase costs. Even accepting the view that 'quality is free'[2], any programme to improve quality is going to incur costs. Many organisations initiate their quality programme with faith that the eventual savings will more than cover the cost of the programme itself. Few make the effort to validate this fact, yet a comparison of the benefits accruing from a quality programme (outputs) with the resources used within the programme (inputs) is, in effect, a form of productivity measure.

Profit and productivity

not what they manage

Productivity is important in that it provides an alternative measure of wellbeing to that of profitability. Profitability, in private sector organisations, is naturally one of the main concerns of senior managers since they have to provide a return to the owners or shareholders. However, profitability can be affected by a number of external factors such as currency fluctuations, price changes on raw materials, etc. Profitability is thus a combination of productivity and 'price recovery' (the net increase in sales volume over increased resource costs). High profitability – especially in the short term – is not a guarantee of long-term stability or success. Profitability can be raised in the short term by increasing prices, but this has limited potential for longer-term success since there is bound to be some consumer resistance to price rises, even for those organisations in a monopoly supply situation. Many monopoly organisations are, in effect, in a competitive situation since they are competing for customers' money with organisations providing other forms of goods and services. Even local authorities are being subjected to competitive pressures in parts of their operation through the process of competitive tendering. Pushing prices even higher simply means that eventually customers will decide that the value they place on the goods is no longer high enough to justify the price; or it means that it increases the opportunities for another organisation to set up in competition. Organisations that also measure their productivity have a measurement which can be used alongside the measurement of profitability to remove the price recovery factors that may be masking true organisational performance; the organisation can thus gain a truer feeling for the current and future wellbeing of the organisation. This is more reliable than simply 'having faith' in the organisation's quality programme.

For those organisations for which profitability is not a valid measure (public and voluntary sector organisations), productivity measurement and improvement can be used as a means of increasing organisational effectiveness. Because of the effect of external factors on profitability, or the lack of profitability as an appropriate measure, productivity remains the best measure of the results of management policies and decisions; in effect, productivity measures the efforts of the management team to improve profitability or organisational effectiveness. This includes the measures of effectiveness of any quality or service programme.)

Productivity has another advantage over profitability. It can be measured at different levels of the organisation, right down to that of the individual employee. At this level profitability would almost certainly be an invalid measure. The overall productivity of the organisation is dependent on the productivity of each division, department, section and individual and it is possible (though not necessarily desirable as we will discuss later) to measure at each level to build a hierarchy of measures that allow analysis of a range of activities and functions that make up the total work of the organisation. So, it can and should be regarded as important. Certainly governments continue to use productivity measures and comparisons in their economic debates and discussions, even though they tend to use productivity figures in their arguments when they feel that they demonstrate the success of their own policies or the failure of their opposition's.

None of the above is exactly original thinking! So why has productivity been so low on the agenda for many organisations? Indeed for many, it has been so low that it has fallen off the bottom of the paper. There are a number of reasons; but one important factor is the blind alley that productivity fell into through continually being equated with labour productivity, and worse, being used as part of the wage bargaining process.

Productivity as a concept was misused and devalued by managers and became mistrusted by employees. In the UK in the 1960s in particular, 'productivity deals' were used, especially in the public sector, to justify wage rises that were above the norms laid down under the prices and incomes legislation. Some of these 'deals' were suspect, to say the least, and although some of them could be demonstrated to improve productivity, that was because productivity was being interpreted on a very narrow basis.

In a time of high employment, productivity tends to be misused in this way since it is used as a bargaining weapon by employers as part of their staff recruitment, retention and remuneration policy. In times of high unemployment, the word becomes once more unacceptable since it has been allowed to gain connotations of job losses. This narrow view of productivity and the way in which it was used within the wage bargaining and industrial relations process gave rise to a number of myths associated with the concept of productivity.[3] These myths are:

- it takes away jobs;

- it only benefits the employer;

- it increases stress and reduces satisfaction;

- it just means working harder;

- it is not appropriate for white collar work.

8

These myths, and the underlying causes, will be examined later; but for now let us just accept that productivity is a much wider concept and is much more widely applicable than has often been regarded in the past.

So, do we need to define it? Perhaps not, but it does ensure that we are all talking about the same thing.

Following through the simple ratio approach, one definition of productivity is that it is 'the relationship between output and one or more of the associated inputs used in the production process.'[4] This definition is important in that it correctly identifies that there are a number of different inputs associated with any output from an industrial or commercial organisation. These inputs are typically labour, capital, and materials, but can include energy and other factors important in particular industrial sectors. In agriculture, for example, commonly quoted statistics relate to the yield of a crop per acre of land cultivated.

One of the problems is that some of these inputs are easier to measure than others. In most organisations, it is relatively easy to get at least an estimate of the labour content of particular activities or processes. It is easy to count people and we normally have to account for the hours they work, their attendance and so on as part of the payment system we use. This is why labour productivity is most commonly discussed and measured. However, in many organisations the labour content of work is diminishing as a proportion of total input. The limits on human capacity also mean that the scope for improved productivity from making people work 'harder' is actually very limited. Thus, concentration on raising labour productivity may not be an effective means of making the whole organisation more 'effective'.

We have now raised once more another of the words that often crop up in any discussion of productivity. The words 'efficiency' and 'effectiveness' are the most common. Effectiveness relates to the ability of an enterprise to meet the goals it has set itself and, thus, productivity increases are important only in so far as they contribute to organisational objectives. It is quite possible to get people to work harder but to reduce effectiveness because they are working on loss-making products or services, or because the work they do results in failures or stoppages later on in a process or procedure.

How and what to measure

Single-factor productivity measures are potentially dangerous – one cannot infer from a measured rise in a single-factor index that beneficial changes have taken place in the area covered by that index. For example, another failing of the concentration on labour productivity is the fact that the ability of labour to produce goods and services is closely related to any changes made to the other input factors. If labour productivity, as measured by a labour productivity index, rises we cannot deduce that the workforce is working harder or is better trained. This may be the case, but output per employee hour can, for example, be much more heavily influenced by changes in capital investment in new plant, machinery and equipment than by changes in working procedures or motivation. Measuring labour productivity only may mask true changes in overall productivity arising from changes in these other factors.

Even where factors other than labour productivity are measured, there is a tendency to concentrate on the productivity of production. In many organisations, the overall performance may be more influenced by what happens in the marketing or distribution areas; concentrating on the production area may offer information on only part of the full picture.

Table 1.1   Output per employee 1960–88

	Average annual % change		
	1960–70	*1970–80*	*1980–88*
UK	2.4	1.3	2.5
USA	2.0	0.4	1.2
Japan	8.9	3.8	2.9
West Germany	4.4	2.8	1.8
France	4.6	2.8	2.0
Italy	6.3	2.6	2.0
Canada	2.4	1.5	1.4
Average	3.5	1.7	1.8

A case is often made that the UK underwent a positive transformation in labour productivity in the 1980s. Table 1.1[5] was used by the Treasury in 1989 as evidence of the 'economic miracle' that has transformed the UK economy. Before a judgement on the figures is made, we need to know something more about the nature of such productivity measures and in particular the limitations of them. Selecting a given set of figures to 'prove a point' is always an exercise fraught with difficulty. The advantage of the figures in Table 1.1 is that they do cover a lengthy period of time and thus presumably show a long-term trend. Productivity is a long-term issue. As in many other areas it is quite possible for short-term, apparently beneficial, results to mask a longer-term, underlying problem.

Table 1.2[5] shows the comparative figures for manufacturing industry only. Here, the results look even more impressive. However, manufacturing in the UK now accounts for only about one job in four (and the proportion is falling), and yet it can be argued that it is these jobs that do most to increase the wealth of the nation. Productivity growth, though welcome, in a declining manufacturing sector does not give rise to confidence for the longer-term future. In fact this decline in the manufacturing sector may itself explain the reported rise in productivity. This is due to the 'batting average concept'.[6] Productivity at national level, which is an aggregate of the performances of individual organisations, is increased by removing the results of low performing organisations from the aggregate as they cease to exist.

Table 1.2 Output per employee (manufacturing industry) 1960–88

	Average annual % change		
	1960–70	*1970–80*	*1980–88*
UK	3.0	1.6	5.2
USA	3.5	3.0	4.0
Japan	8.8	5.3	3.1
West Germany	4.1	2.9	2.2
France	5.4	3.2	3.1
Italy	5.4	3.0	3.5
Canada	3.4	3.0	3.6
Average	4.5	3.3	3.6

An alternative productivity study produced in 1988 by the PA Consulting Group in conjunction with the Confederation of British Industry and using OECD figures gives another comparison of long-term productivity growth among the leading industrial nations. These trends are shown in Figure 1.1.

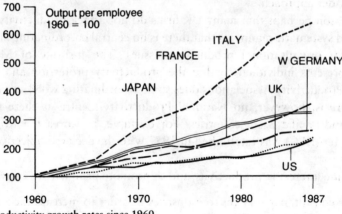

Figure 1.1 Productivity growth rates since 1960.

Improving productivity

The position of the UK now looks comparatively worse. Although UK productivity (in terms of output per employee) has been rising since 1960, it started from a lower base than many of the country's competitors, and to reach the same 'absolute' levels, the UK needs to achieve what at first sight are probably impossible rates of growth. However, Tom Peters[7] suggests that productivity increases of 200 or 300 per cent are not impossible targets.

There is also evidence that much of the improvement in productivity has been achieved at the expense of higher rates of unemployment. Organisations throughout the 1980s have been shedding their excess labour. While this should give the UK 'leaner, fitter' organisations more able to compete with external competitors, it must be seen as a 'one-off' exercise achieved perhaps painfully but relatively simply. To continue the trend is going to require much more systematic and targeted programmes attacking other areas and factors affecting the productivity ratio.

From the above discussion we can see that the major myths are:

- productivity is about production;
- productivity is about labour;
- productivity is about working harder;
- improving productivity means cutting costs;
- increased productivity means redundancy.

These myths have led to productivity being treated in a mechanistic, isolated way. Almost always, only the production function is subjected to any kind of review or study; and this will usually be limited to a review of labour productivity. The real potential for productivity improvement cannot be realised in this way. It requires a fuller and wider approach.

One reason perhaps that many UK firms do not attack productivity in a more effective and systematic manner is that there is no central co-ordinating and promoting force for organisational productivity issues. The Institute of Management Services represents individuals within the productivity profession and the British Council of Productivity Associations does some co-ordinating work among organisations. There is, however, no National Productivity Centre as there is in many European and Pacific Basin countries. For example, in Korea the Korean Productivity Center (KPC) was established in 1957 with the declared objectives:

- to stimulate interest in productivity and to promote productivity consciousness;
- to render consultancy services to industries in order to increase their managerial and operational effectiveness;
- to train industrial personnel to improve their productivity;
- to collect and disseminate information relating to productivity improvement;
- to act as the integrated focal point of all organisations engaged in the productivity improvement drive.

One example of their approach is a nation-wide productivity drive, the 'Double Productivity Movement', launched in 1989 with the aim of doubling added value productivity within a five-year period. This drive is supported with promotional materials, training materials, advisory programmes and information exchange programmes. Similar centres exist in many of the countries of south-east Asia, countries which are rapidly becoming major competitors of the developed Western nations.

The nearest the UK has to such organisations is the various development agencies that exist in particular areas. For example, the Scottish Borders Enterprise Agency has declared aims of:

- improving productivity;
- increasing the competitiveness of local industry;
- increasing the customer orientation;
- ensuring a quality service;
- attacking world markets.

In the absence of such promotional and 'missionary' work provided by a national centre, it is left to such agencies and to individual organisations to address their own productivity issues as best they see fit. If the UK is to remain a major industrial and commercial force, and is to continue to improve the standards of living and the quality of life of its population, then the issue of improving productivity must be addressed by a greater number of organisations; and it must be done in a broad, all-factor-encompassing manner. It must address the productivity of all resources: land, buildings, materials, energy, machines, equipment and manpower. The concept of productivity must be communicated to all those who influence it and are influenced by it.

Quality has a part to play within productivity, as we shall see in the next chapter. It is one of the number of factors, perhaps the most important (though it can be regarded as a subset of 'value'), that the customer/client expects to receive from the product/service supplier. However, it is an external factor, based on these customer perceptions. The organisation providing products or services must provide quality, but it must do so at an appropriate level that ensures its profitability, survival or wellbeing. Quality is thus the customer's aim; productivity is the organisation's. An attempt to attack one of these aims without the other is addressing only part of the overall success scenario.

This book is an attempt to spread the message of the importance of productivity; to link productivity improvement to the new moves in quality and service improvement; and to offer information and guidance to organisations who may 'see the light' but not be sure how to turn it on!

Tomorrow may be too late to start thinking of improving our productivity!

Keynotes
Economic growth is dependent on productivity growth. Productivity growth increases the size of the 'cake'; otherwise, it can only be redistributed.

13

Productivity is the only secure way of increasing the standard of living, of improving a nation's balance of payments, of controlling inflation and of providing more leisure time.

High profitability (especially in the short term) is not a guarantee of long-term stability or success. Organisations who also measure their productivity have a measurement which can be used alongside the measurement of profitability to get a truer feeling for the current and future wellbeing of the organisation.

Productivity measures the efforts of the management team to improve profitability or organisational effectiveness.

Effectiveness relates to the ability of an enterprise to meet the goals it has set itself, and thus productivity increases are important only in so far as they contribute to organisational objectives.

Productivity is a long-term issue. As in many other areas, it is quite possible for short-term, apparently beneficial, results to mask a longer-term, underlying problem. Productivity must therefore be addressed on a continuing basis over a long period of time.

Quality is the customer's aim; productivity is the supplying organisation's.

Tomorrow may be too late to start thinking of improving our productivity!

Discussion topics
At an organisational level, productivity must be measured in multifactor terms since the resources being consumed by an organisation may consist of land, buildings, energy, capital and people. At a national level, however, the other factors are, by and large, constant and thus it is only necessary to measure labour productivity.

The 'quality revolution' simply distracts attention away from the fundamental productivity problem and can therefore be considered as a harmful and damaging influence.

Since there are no internationally agreed mechanisms for measuring and comparing productivity, it is dangerous to draw conclusions from published productivity figures for different nations or organisations.

References
1 *'Introduction to work study'*, 3rd edition (1979). Geneva: International Labour Organisation.

2 Crosby, Philip (1979) *Quality is free*. New York: McGraw-Hill.

3 Dahl, T. (1986). University of Minnesota. Paper to the World Productivity Congress, Indonesia.

4 *Measurement and interpretation of productivity* (1979). Washington, DC: National Research Council, National Academy of Sciences.

5 Callaghan, W. (1990) 'Productivity for profit', *Work Study*, Vol. 39 No. 2, pp. 6–19, March/April.

6 Burgess, T. (1990) 'A review of productivity', *Work Study*, Vol. 39 No. 1, pp. 6–9, Jan/Feb.

7 Peters, T. J. and Waterman, R. H. Jnr (1982) *In search of excellence*. New York: Harper & Row.

2 Top-line productivity

The discussion on productivity in the previous chapter concentrated on the bottom-line figure of the productivity ratio, on the need to make better use of the resources consumed by organisations – both, in terms of self-interest, to make them more efficient and, taking a global view, to conserve vital natural resources. Similarly, nearly all productivity improvement programmes carried out in UK industry are seen as essentially bottom-line, cost-reduction exercises. Many of these are successful and provide real productivity gains. However, it is obvious that an 'improvement' in the value of a ratio can be obtained by changing either the top or bottom lines (or both together, naturally). Why has the top line been given so little attention?

There are a number of reasons. One seems to be that costs are associated with 'waste' and thus perceived as the main target for attack. Culturally, we in the UK are trained to think of waste as almost sinful, perhaps as a legacy from World War II where resources had to be consumed with care. Similarly after the war there was a need to re-establish non-war-related manufacturing and the aim was to get goods out to customers as quickly as possible. Resources were limited and thus productivity was important – in terms of making good use of available and limited resources, especially labour. Thus, the equating of productivity improvement with cost reduction in general and labour productivity in particular began. Although the war ended over 45 years ago, it is still a powerful memory for many of those now in senior management positions. For many managers, their formative years were spent in organisations and in a time when labour costs were the biggest proportion of total costs. Also, costs are easily measured and have to be measured in most organisations as part of the normal accounting function. Thus, data are readily available on which to base simple single-factor productivity indices.

The drive for quality has hit the UK particularly late. Again, perhaps because the UK had a 'head start' on most of the other manufacturing nations, its industry was content to concentrate on output quantity in the belief that the market would be there, ready and waiting. For a long time this was undoubtedly true.

Another major reason for concentration on cost reduction is that in a time of growth, many organisations are content to increase output, not quite at all costs but certainly with little regard to the balance between the increased output and the increased costs of producing that output. The growth itself 'finances' the additional output. Thus, often a high rate of growth is accompanied by a lowering of some productivity factors. Increased capital investment that often accompanies growth may raise overall productivity, but little attention is paid to, say, labour or energy efficiency. A number of smaller organisations when going through their main growth phase are at their most vulnerable. Either they start to experience cashflow or under-resourcing problems, or they allow their inputs to rise in an uncontrolled manner. Growth kills as many organisations as does a recession.

For those organisations who manage to survive the growth phase, the slowing down or full cessation of growth brings other problems. The management of the organisation begins to look for 'savings' that can finance the potential contraction and starts to readdress the productivity ratio: in this case, the only improvement that can be made is by attacking the input part of the ratio. One ironic by-product of this urge to reduce costs in a time of contraction or recession is that one of the first things that often happens is that service functions are often curtailed or eliminated. This may include those service functions which would normally carry out or assist in productivity improvement programmes.

This rightly reminds us that organisations will treat the concept of productivity differently at different stages in their development. The quality revolution being experienced (or at least promoted) is essenntially aimed at stable organisations who have largely attacked productivity in the traditional way: by cutting costs and increasing efficiencies. Thus a <u>common sequence for productivity improvement</u> is:

- Ignore productivity – other issues are too important.
- Concentrate on labour productivity to contain costs.
- Attack process efficiency.
- Review product productivity – evaluate the product range, standardisation of components, etc.
- Ignore productivity and examine other ways of adding value – quality, service, etc.

Naturally these stages are not mutually exclusive; there is no reason why an organis-ation should not keep all aspects of its operation under review at the same time. However, it is rather like a novice golfer. There are so many things to remember about the golf swing – the stance, the grip, the takeaway of the club, the cocking of the wrists, transferring the weight between the feet, keeping the head still, and so on – that it is generally confusing and counterproductive to concentrate on more than one or two at any one time. The organisation can address several issues but the existing forms of structure adopted by most organisations is not suitable to address labour, product, process and 'other' issues simultaneously. Thus the organisation inevitably has a major drive in one particular area or attempts to cover a number by assigning different ones to different individuals or groups (there is a management services department which addresses certain issues, the quality department addresses

17

that one issue, costs are the responsibility of the finance department and so on). The trouble with such an approach is that it can lead to suboptimisation, in which one area is improved to the detriment of another or to the overall operation.

Another factor which ensures that productivity retains a narrow focus is the influence within UK industry of the accountant. More than in any other country, the accountant or financial manager tends to dominate boardroom discussions. The UK trains far more accountants than other developed nations and allows them to rise much faster within even manufacturing organisations than, say, the engineers responsible for actually making the goods. Although it would be unfair to denigrate the whole of the accountancy profession, there has been a tendency to concentrate on what is easily counted and measured and to pay too much attention to short-term futures at the expense of the longer term. (This also affects the investment policies of both companies and share-buying individuals and agencies; everyone seems to want a quick return.) The number of accountants in the UK, and the number of other professionals, such as lawyers, means that there are too many people involved in the redistribution of the cake and not enough concerned with baking a bigger one! If an organisation is truly committed to productivity improvement, it should demonstrate it (in one way) by ensuring that production and productivity matters are represented at board of director level. In the UK there are basically two cultures: those of the arts and the sciences. In parts of Europe, and especially Germany, there is a third culture, that of 'Technik', which values the ability to make.

The organisation should also make some attempt to concentrate the minds of its senior managers on longer-term issues rather than on the share price this month or the next quarter's profit figures. This switch of attitude can be accomplished by linking the pay (or part of it) of senior managers to the productivity improvements achieved over a longer time span. This may also serve as a retention mechanism for key senior staff, enabling longer-term planning to be carried out in the knowledge that those responsible for the planning are likely to be around when the results become visible.

Two lessons follow from the above. Firstly, if real and continuing gains are to be made, a longer-term and more systematic approach to productivity improvement should be taken, one which addresses the full range of factors involved (including top-line factors); and, secondly, productivity should be a constant agenda item, not pulled 'out of the hat' when the organisation is in trouble.

Top-line factors

The reference to 'top-line factors' raises the important issue that not only do most organisations give too much attention to the bottom-line (input) factors, but also that the top line is generally interpreted as being a simple measure of output, expressed in terms of some basic unit. This equating of 'output' with simple quantitative measures of throughput is the reason for the missed opportunities of productivity improvement. Increasing the top line of the productivity ratio is almost always interpreted as increasing the throughput of the organisation in terms of numbers produced. For many organisations, the state of the market in terms of total size and market share means that increased throughput cannot be easily delivered to the marketplace; the tendency is therefore to concentrate on maintaining existing throughput levels but attempting to do so with fewer input resources.

However, customers do not buy quantity. They are not, in most cases, concerned with how many of our goods we can produce or what level of our service we can maintain. Quantity is, of course, important to customers in that it generally governs availability (and it may affect the costs we incur and hence the price we charge) but it is not an important issue in helping the customer or client select our offering as compared to that of our competitors. Some of our customers may buy 'in quantity' but their decision is more complex than simply finding a supplier who can offer the quantity they require.

Organisations provide goods or services in return for some form of payment from their customers or clients. Most operate in some kind of competitive environment in which the customer selects the goods or services on the basis of some, perhaps unknown, criteria which are often aggregated into the concept of 'value'. Thus the output of the organisation is aimed at meeting a subset of the possible criteria which are identified as being important (offering value) in the chosen market. This is a marketing decision. If we consider manufactured goods, the major criteria can be identified as:

- functionality;
- performance;
- quality;
- durability;
- reliability;
- aesthetics;
- size;
- weight;
- cost;
- life-cycle costs (maintenance, consumables, etc.).

with perhaps just as important, though less 'physical', criteria being:

- status;
- fashion; and
- availability.

Naturally not all goods will possess each of the criteria, and not all organisations will address each of the criteria with the same degree of priority. Engineering goods for example, may not be subject to the whims of fashion, while others, such as, say, perfume, will not be assigned 'functionality'. However, it must be realised that the output of any organisation is much more than a simple quantitative throughput.

The marketing policy of a given organisation may be to attack a particular market segment by a low price strategy, and to achieve this they may pay less attention to certain other criteria. It is also likely that organisations may change their policy as they mature; perhaps as a start-up venture they may have to adopt and promote a particular criterion as a means of gaining market penetration; as the market position stabilises, the organisation may decide to change the balance of established criteria to reach new markets or to change the perceived company and/or product/service image.

One recent example of this approach has been the Amstrad range of computers. See Case example 2.1.

Case example 2.1

Amstrad started by offering low-price computers to a previously untapped market. It did this very successfully by identifying basic functionality and providing it in an effective, low-cost package. The reason for its outstanding success was that the machines it provided offered an acceptable level of functionality, performance and reliability at an acceptable price – a price which brought computers into a market which previously had considered them out of reach. Those who bought early versions of the machines passed on recommendations and, though the corporate world was reluctant at first to buy computers from such an 'unknown' source (with its past reputation based largely on cheap hi-fi equipment), the continuing good reports and good reviews from the technical press slowly got these machines into companies as well as into homes.

However, a number of other companies had seen (though not quite as soon) the same market opportunity and the number of cheap computers in competition started to proliferate.

Amstrad attempted to move 'up-market' by offering additional functionality and improved performance (and perhaps status) in a new range of machines. Unfortunately its first efforts were marred by reduced reliability, and the fact that its 'output' in terms of quantity of goods available for sale was insufficient to meet a significant percentage of the perceived market did not help Amstrad gain the market penetration it was seeking. In all such marketing moves luck plays a part and unfortunately Amstrad made its 'up-market' move just as a shortage of memory chips hit the general computing market. These were the very chips that Amstrad needed for its new machines. This was a major reason for its inability to produce in sufficient quantities, but the faults in the early machines were more damaging in the long term. Its output was affected negatively, both quantitatively and qualitatively.

The effects on Amstrad's image as a 'productive' organisation were reflected in the decline in its share price.

Other factors

In some markets, the purchase price paid by the consumer may be a relatively unimportant factor when compared to some of the other criteria. Certainly, the 'value' of goods or services as perceived by the consumer may change much more rapidly with changes in other criteria than with changes in purchase price. This is true even where financial considerations are uppermost in the minds of potential purchasers. For example, much expensive machinery – such as mainframe computers – carries ongoing maintenance costs, which over the life of the machine may incur costs that are more significant to the organisation than the initial purchase price. Technological changes which reduce these ongoing costs may be regarded as much more important than a reduction in the purchase price. (When the 'typical' family motorcar moved from three-month to six-month service intervals, those manufacturers who introduced the change first were able to use this as a major selling point – a competitive edge.) This is especially true in certain markets, such as some of those in the public sector, where a clear distinction is made between capital and revenue spending. For instance, it may be possible to spend capital monies obtained by way of grant from a government agency, research body, etc. on equipment, but the revenue implications of maintenance and consumable costs may have to be borne out of a revenue budget which is not automatically increased to take account of such costs.

Thus, there are at least two alternative strategies for market penetration: the low-cost strategy and the product differentiation strategy. Product differentiation may result in higher costs in order to produce more non-standard goods and for the higher advertising and promotion activities that may be required to convince customers that the product is indeed different from that of competitors, but should increase revenue through the price premium that the differentiated products will attract. Both strategies, if successful at improving sales and market share, should ultimately lead to some cost reduction in terms of providing economies of scale. Product differentiation may additionally increase the size of the potential market.[1] The effects of alternative strategies in terms of productivity are complex, but productivity improvement can be achieved by both strategies.

Output is therefore, something different than throughput and productivity is more than throughput over cost. Output is a complex amalgam of the above criteria and the output of a given organisation is a particular 'output mix'. The Amstrad lesson also reminds us that first offerings and first impressions are important but, in many sectors, an ongoing reputation and track record is essential to break into the large markets.

The intention of most organisations is to create a favourable output mix which differentiates their goods or services from those of competitors' and hopefully allows a large-volume market to develop or allows a premium price to be charged. Sometimes this differentiation by the consumer can be the result of very small differences in the quality of goods or level of service, as in Case example 2.2.

The importance of the 'smallness' of improvements should not be overlooked.

Case example 2.2

Hotel guests often order morning newspapers. These are generally delivered and left outside the guests' hotel doors, so as not to disturb them. The papers are often labelled with the room number to ensure correct delivery and so that guests can confirm that they have received the right paper.

Some hotels label the paper with the guests' names to offer a 'personal' touch. However, this is often simply a surname written with a ball-point pen. Recently, I was in a hotel that took the trouble to wrap the newspaper in a sleeve which had a compliments message and my full name printed on it. This is a small, extra-value item but is evidence of the hotel's attempt to convey an air of quality of service.

Small grows and small adds, and a number of small improvements or additional offerings can create a large impact on the end-consumer. This is comparable to the case of top athletes where, in the 100 metres for example, a tiny margin separates the very best from the merely good. Yet the best are clearly identified as such. As well as a growing benefit, smallness also grows confidence in both the management and the workforce – who see small suggestions and small decisions being taken seriously and making a significant contribution. The seriousness with which small matters are treated strengthens commitment to improvement of all aspects of the operation.

Obviously additional service or additional product features may incur additional cost. The intention of addressing the top-line factors is not to offer over-lavish additions to existing provision but to consider ways in which that existing provision may be produced, packaged or presented more effectively.

If we think of productivity as the ratio of the output mix to the inputs that create it, we arrive at a much more complex ratio but one with much more scope for development and improvement. The increased scope arises from the number of, and the importance of, these top-line factors. That is not to say that organisations should stop attempting to monitor, control and reduce their inputs but that the ratio should be considered on both sides. Top-line productivity is thus:

- the amalgam of 'top-line factors' compared to the aggregation of resource inputs.

This concept holds true at all levels. One of the attractions of this new definition which incorporates the customer/client/consumer perception of value through the top-line factors, is that it allows the term 'productivity' to be used in a much more flexible, imaginative and useful way. For example, the 'greening' of society through increasing concern for the environmental effects of industrial and commercial processes, means that increased throughput or more efficient throughput may be regarded as inappropriate if the level of environmental damage is proportionally increased. The concept of top-line productivity allows the inclusion of such factors in discussions of productivity. Thus an environmentally friendly product, such as organically grown vegetables, may attract a price premium but may be considered as good value for money in the eyes of a significant part of the potential market. Taking this range of factors and bearing in mind the traditional approach to productivity measurement and improvement outlined in Chapter 1, we can see that there is a large variety of routes to improved productivity – routes which affect all sectors and departments of an organisation. In fact, this is one of the major strengths of a productivity improvement programme that is concerned with this 'top-line productivity' – it must be a total team effort involving all functions and all personnel within the organisation. Productivity can thus be improved by:

- *improved product/service design* to increase the output through improved functionality, reliability or aesthetic appearance;

- *improved manufacturing processes and procedures* which can attack either or both of the parts of the productivity ratio: the numerator by implementing process or procedural change which leads to improved quality or reliability of goods, and the denominator by reducing costs and wastage;

- *increased capital investment* to improve manufacturing or delivery processes;

- *improved labour performance* to reduce manufacturing/delivery costs;

- *increased levels of labour participation/involvement* to assist in the improvement of quality and labour performance;

- *more effective research and development* to increase output by providing better products and services, and processes;

and so on. Productivity is not an issue for the manufacturers only – it must be addressed by everyone.

Productivity improvement programmes

We mentioned in Chapter 1 that in agriculture, productivity may be measured by the yield of a crop per acre. Traditional productivity improvement techniques concentrate on improving the yield. However, a top-line productivity improvement programme would also consider the changing of the crop to one which offers a higher return.

Organisations who wish to improve their top-line productivity must do so with an all-embracing improvement programme. This programme may be called a top-line productivity programme, a quality programme, a business review, or any one of a host of other names. The name assigned to the programme is important only in so far as it is part of the communication process used to 'sell' the concept to the members of the organisation: the name chosen should be one which it is felt will appeal to and enthuse all levels of the workforce. Throughout the rest of this book we will continue to use the terms 'top-line productivity' and 'top-line productivity improvement programme'.

Although using this concept of top-line productivity enables us to attack productivity improvement in a much wider way, it leaves us with a major problem. How do we measure this 'top-line productivity'?

First we should ask the question of whether productivity measurement is important. One school of thought suggests that without measurement it is difficult to control and to set targets for future activity and improvement. Some would go as far as to say that if a factor cannot be measured, then it should be excluded from serious consideration.[2] Another school of thought suggests that measurement itself is restricting – in creating targets that form 'norms' and prevent the pursuit of excellence. There is room for measurement as an aid to planning and controlling but it must be used with care.

Can all the top-line criteria be measured? The answer to that depends on what we mean by measurement. We have already stated that customers or clients evaluate such criteria in some way in their perception of value. They may not use precise measuring techniques or measurement scales but they do make some judgement of the relative content or magnitude of each criterion when comparing one set of goods or services with another. The recognition that this judgement takes place is vital to understanding the concept of top-line productivity.

If customers and clients are going to make judgements on the nature of the goods and services we offer, then we should do it first. The fact that we cannot measure some of the factors with a watch, a ruler, a weighing machine or any other simple device does not mean that some form of measurement cannot be undertaken. In fact, measures of many of the criteria mentioned above are made regularly by market researchers. When companies are testing market reaction to new products, it is common to carry out consumer testing through a number of devices and to make some assessment of the consumer's judgement on such difficult-to-measure issues as style, aesthetics and image and to combine these assessments with more 'scientific' measurements of such things as reliability and quality which may be tested and assessed numerically in some form of laboratory environment. Although some of these measurements are 'subjective', this does not matter. Or alternatively, they become even more important since it is often subjective measures that determine the customer's reaction to our products. It is important that we recognise the kind of decision-making process undertaken by our potential customers and clients and evaluate our goods and services in the same manner. It is dangerous to assume that we know what affects the buying decisions of our customers. See Case example 2.3.

Quality care
There have been a number of companies that have recently introduced quality or customer care campaigns of one sort or another. Such programmes will be discussed in detail in following chapters but essentially they are both attempts to change the

---

Case example 2.3

An airline collected together some of its staff and asked them to list the factors that would attract customers to that airline in preference to another and which would be regarded as evidence of 'good service'. The staff came up with a list of factors such as:

Customers want the plane to leave on time.

Customers want an efficient, friendly check-in service.

Customers want their baggage to be handled quickly and safely.

Customers want a clean and pleasant terminal building.

A separate exercise was undertaken with customers themselves. It turned out that all the above factors were within the basic expectations of customers and were thus indicators of competence of basic service. They did not earn the company additional merit. The customers were looking for something extra and cited such things as:

I want to be treated as something more than a number on the flight list.

I expect special provision for the elderly, infirm or children.

I would like 'proper' crockery and cutlery.

I would like good information about the flight path.

---

corporate culture and attitude to ensure that the requirements and expectations of customers or clients are the driving forces behind the product or service delivery. Generally quality management programmes perform that task in manufacturing organisations, and customer care programmes in service organisations, although there is a degree of overlap.

Although many organisations naturally are aware of the inter-relationship between these two areas of concern, rarely do we see an attempt to combine the two (and other initiatives) in a systematic manner and address them as part of the wider issue of improved productivity. They are often addressed as 'an act of faith' in the hope that concentration on quality or customer care will lead to improved customer take-up of and loyalty to the targeted product or service. Such acts of faith are mostly successful, assuming the quality (or other) campaigns are organised and handled well, but they do have their limitations. Many of the campaigns lose impetus after a few months. Exhortation is a short-term motivating force. Quality circle programmes, for example, may require individual circles to be 'rested' for periods of time to avoid circle meetings at which employees simply 'go through the motions'. The time taken between changes made as a result of such programmes and the benefits being demonstrated in financial results may be quite long. For organisations in which financial results are not the best indicator of success, the situation is even worse. There is no adequate recognition of success or even progress being made. Productivity – and especially top-line productivity – measurement can offer such measures of progress to maintain commitment and impetus.

This acceptance of quality or customer care as another means of improving competitiveness or raising profit, is also carried out by some organisations rather as if they were changing the window display of their shop. In order to be successful, such campaigns must receive total commitment from the senior management of the organisation and become part of the culture and philosophy of an organisation. Deming himself (perhaps the most famous of the quality 'gurus') has said that American managers use quality circles as a lazy way to avoid the job of improving quality and productivity.[3]

An indication of the failure of UK management to address productivity in this top-line sense, and to co-ordinate improvements in efficiency and cost saving with improvements in the top-line factors, is given in a recent survey undertaken by the Institute of Management Services of organisations across the UK.[4] Of organisations questioned, 80 per cent answered 'yes' to the question:[6] 'Is your company implementing a productivity improvement programme?' Yet, of those who answered in the affirmative, only 56 per cent claimed that the quality of goods/services had been improved through the programme, and 41 per cent said that the productivity improvement programme had no effect on quality.

Meaningful programmes of quality or productivity improvement cannot happen overnight. Major change (and to be effective, it must be a major change) needs adequate preparation and carefully controlled implementation. This is what the Japanese do well.

Staff development

There is a considerable amount of staff development to be undertaken – both in terms of training in any specific techniques involved, and in terms of the attitudinal changes required. UK industry, in particular, has a poor record of training and a much worse one of employee development. This raises another reason for the lack of success of quality or customer care programmes. In Japan, all employees are regarded as potential managers and are trained and developed to a high degree. In Japanese quality circles, for example, extensive use may be made of statistical quality control charts and such techniques as Pareto analysis, secure in the knowledge that the workforce has the necessary training to understand and use them. In the UK, this attitude is most unlikely. Training, if done at all, will be restricted to the very immediate demands of the individual's job.

There is also often a simplistic (and often mistaken) belief that because something is successful in one place and at one time, it is likely to be so at another place or another time. This is one of the charges levelled at some of the management consulting firms who specialise in particular techniques. One view is that such consultants are hawking around their solutions looking for problems that can be squeezed into them. Often though, the place to where the 'solution' is transplanted has a different problem or a different environment. Where, as is the case with quality circles, the transplant is done between radically different cultures, the chance of success, especially in the short term, is very low. Thus we should look at transplanting ideas and concepts, but look to implement on our own terms, at our own pace and according to our own situation. This is what the Japanese did with the Deming philosophy.

We should be building our own tailored programme of improvement, whether it be for customer care, quality or any other attribute. However, if we do take a single attribute such as customer care or quality to promote and improve, we are in danger of simply following the latest fashion, or in 'pushing problems further down the line'.

The advantage of including such issues in a top-line productivity improvement campaign is that it allows a number of inter-related issues to be addressed as part of a concerted, ongoing effort; and the measurement and reporting inherent in a structured programme provides the target setting and monitoring essential to mount a long-term control programme. It won't guarantee immediate results but it should be possible to make enough short-term gains to 'finance' the longer-term commitment necessary for longer-term development and success, and to gain the real – and large – benefits accruing from the continuing and continual commitment.

Top-line productivity is about designing and implementing productive methods and procedures and ensuring that the employees who use them do so in a productive manner. It is not about finding the faults and imposing solutions on an unwilling or uncooperative workforce but in working together with that workforce to build an organisation that treats them with respect and uses their enthusiasm and interest in partnership with management to build a high-productivity organisation with benefits for all.

Of course, some organisations in the UK are attacking productivity in a systematic and meaningful way. The National Productivity Award in the UK, which is jointly sponsored by the Institute of Management Services and the British Council of Productivity Associations, examines the productivity improvement schemes and results of a number of companies and organisations. The finalists represent those organisations who have had major success in improving their productivity. These, however, represent only a few of the large number of organisations who must improve their productivity if industry, commerce and the public sector between them are to increase national wealth and improve competitiveness in international markets. Success among an enthusiastic few is not enough. Productivity analysis and improvement must be taken on board by the great mass of organisations, in all sectors, whether they be large or small. If they treat the concept widely enough and use the full armoury of approaches and techniques available, and if they do it with true participative commitment on an ongoing basis, then the UK will start to catch up with its immediate competitors and strengthen its position in the international marketplace.

Keynotes

There has been a tendency to concentrate on what is easily counted and measured, and to pay too much attention to short-term futures at the expense of the longer term.

The output of any organisation is much more than a simple quantitative throughput.

Top-line productivity is the amalgam of 'top-line factors' compared to the aggregation of resource inputs.

Exhortation is a short-term motivating force.

Customers/clients evaluate top-line factors in some way in their perception of value.

Meaningful programmes of quality or productivity improvement cannot happen overnight. Major change (and to be effective, it must be a major change) needs adequate preparation and carefully controlled implementation.

Top-line productivity improvement is not about finding the faults and imposing solutions on an unwilling or uncooperative workforce but in working together with that workforce to build an organisation that treats them with respect and uses their enthusiasm and interest in partnership with management to build a high-productivity organisation with benefits for all.

Discussion topics

The last time you made a major purchase (car, washing machine, television, etc.), what were the criteria by which you judged competing offerings? Are there any factors you have since discovered in the product that you would like changing or enhancing?

Within your own sphere of activity (at home, at work, at leisure), who are your 'customers' (to whom do you provide some form of service)? Are those services provided in a consistent manner? How could they be improved at little cost – (money, time, effort)?

Only a small percentage of the population ever attend live theatre performances. If you were a theatre manager, what steps would you take to attract the remainder of the population? Of these steps, how many are concerned with the product (the shows staged) and how many with the overall service?

References

1 Gareth, J. and Butler, J. (1988) 'Costs, revenue and business-level strategy', *Academy of Management Review*, Vol. 13 No. 2, pp. 202–213, April.

2 Reddin, W. (1989) *The output oriented manager*, Aldershot: Gower.

3 'The roots of quality control in Japan', *Pacific Basin Quarterly*, No. 12, Spring/Summer 1985, Pacific Basin Center Foundation, Palo Alto, California.

4 'Productivity and quality in the '90s' (1990), *Management Services*, Vol. 34 No. 6, pp. 28–32, June.

3 The effects of uncertainty

Most of us will recognise from our own experience both in our own organisations and outside of them that the rate of change of the environment seems to move ever upwards. The world continues to shrink with ever-improving communications technologies and the differences between parts of the world are constantly being eroded. This was brought sharply into focus with the 1989/90 changes in Eastern Europe – changes that were far more dramatic and much faster than anyone predicted. On a more local basis, it is evidenced by the standardisation of the high street and the shopping mall. Wherever you go throughout the UK, it is the same shops with the same displays of the same products that greet you.

Commercial organisations face increasing competition from other parts of the world and may be forced into alliances with former competitors to meet a stronger, external threat. Public sector organisations continue to face changing legislation which radically affects the ways in which their services are financed and organised. Education is in turmoil: in the last few years, schools have been faced with implementing the 16+ examination, which was rapidly withdrawn so that the GCE and CSE exams could be replaced with the GCSE; they are currently implementing parts of the new national curriculum, records of achievement, local management of schools and other initiatives.

The past was concerned with increasing standardisation. Organisations became larger so that they could take advantage of economies of scale, which they did by providing a limited range of products across wide markets. Now, in spite of the standardisation of the high street, we are moving into an age of increasing diversification. The consumer is king; rising disposable incomes have resulted in consumers selecting goods and services which are differentiated from standard offerings. See Case example 3.1.

Although we still have big organisations offering goods across larger and often international markets, there has been a realisation that different cultural backgrounds require different, or varied, product and service offerings. The motorcar market is one of the most international, with models being built in one country for sale in several others. Yet, especially in the UK, there is a strong demand for a range of versions of any one model and for a range of extras with which an individual car may be customised. A relatively basic car, such as a Ford Fiesta, may be added to with optional extras to the point where it costs as much as a BMW.

Case example 3.1

McDonald's, the epitome of the standard product/service offering, has realised that its standards do not meet all eventualities and all markets. Though it continues to grow by opening new stores in all parts of the globe (such as Moscow) it is also examining its range of offering. The McDonald's in Rome, for example, is not the lookalike store we normally expect – presumably because the Rome planners laid down constraints – and offers a salad bar not found in the typical McDonald's store. Back home, in the USA, McDonald's is experimenting with pizzas to cope with increasing competition in the fast-food market.

Retail organisations now change their stock about six times each year, whereas 20 years ago they had two main seasons. The effect on the number of product lines is astonishing – there are major problems of getting enough products to meet the increased number of seasons and the project management involved in disposing of one stock range and replacing it with another in such a short timescale gives retailers a number of headaches.

Product life-cycles have become extremely short in many areas, especially those of high technology. The changes that occur are, however, not all associated with technological change. This year's pocket calculator or digital watch has different, and almost certainly more, functions than last year's but could probably have been made last year. Many of the changes are marketing rather than technical changes.

The changes have been categorised as 'additive innovation'; for example, adding to existing product ranges by offering greater variety of product type, size, colour, etc., and 'substitutive innovation'; for example, replacing existing products, technologies, processes and procedures.[1]

External change, as it affects industrial and commercial organisations, occurs in:

- government policy and practice;

- legislation;

- the industrial, national and international standards setting process;

- the society in which the organisation operates
  — nationally;
  — locally;

- economic and labour market conditions
  — globally;
  — nationally;
  — locally;

- available technologies;

and these changes, in turn, result in changes to markets, profit margins, acceptable employment policies, and so on.

Implications of change

The unknown nature and amount of change makes it difficult to cope with and even where the nature and pace of change is known, there will be unknown implications. The coming of the Single European Market was heralded well in advance; there was a definite timescale to it; it was given extensive publicity, advice was freely available; yet many organisations could not interpret the effects it would have on them. The change was certain; the effects remained uncertain. A survey carried out in the summer of 1990 by the Small Business Research Trust on behalf of the National Westminster Bank[2] indicated that most of the 1,200 respondents had considered the implications of the Single Market but that around a third had opted for a 'wait and see' policy before making decisions. The reasons for inaction most often cited were the perceived lack of information and an uncertainty of how the changes would affect the firm. Yet Japanese industry has responded to this well-advertised change with action. Mindful of potential problems, and regulations about importing from outside into this new, large market, they set about creating internal manufacturing centres within the European Community. Change provides opportunities for those perceptive enough to read the advance signs, recognise the change early and to take action to turn it to their own advantage.

The second aspect of change is that the nature of the change is itself becoming more unpredictable and uncertain. If you cast your mind back to predictions made several years ago about the world of today, some of those predictions will be wildly overestimated and some wildly underestimated. Occasionally, the television programme 'Tomorrow's World' carries out a retrospective analysis of past items. Many of the products and ideas shown have sunk without trace; some have been accepted into the mainstream; some have had their time and been overtaken.

This change has a number of effects. There is no doubt that in some areas changes were – and are still – necessary. A world with no change would be unthinkable. People, however, may react to change with a mixture of emotions. Change gives rise to uncertainty in the minds of employees. Even where changes may be perceived as beneficial, there is still an element of fear coupled with uncertainty. There seems in most people to be a basic reluctance to change. Stability is associated with security, and the work of Maslow and others reminds us of the basic need for security. Even those who may welcome change will be wary if it comes too fast or too often.

Some organisations react to resistance to change by avoiding it. In the changing environment we have described above, this is a recipe for disaster. Organisations must change to keep pace with their environments, and should be attempting to predict changes which offer particular opportunities. For example, many successful companies of the last decade have achieved that success by anticipating technological change and capitalising on it – not necessarily by incorporating it into their own activities (though this is obviously a potentially fruitful area), but by offering goods or services which support that technological change. Thus small firms spring up which offer reconditioning of laser printer cartridges, software to cope with legislative change such as the laws relating to COSHH (Control of Substances Hazardous to Health), bar-code printing and so on.

Industry and commerce within the UK seems to pride itself on the fact that it is opportunistic and adaptable. The UK does not have, for example, a formalised system of industrial democracy and participation similar to that of western Germany. There is a tendency to treat each situation anew and to muddle through on the basis of temporary arrangements and local negotiation. Although by and large this works, there is often wasted effort and wasted opportunity. Little attention is paid to conceptual thinking and to careful forecasting and planning. Uncertainty requires a structure and procedures that anticipate change and prepare for ways to deal with it.

This means, naturally, that organisations must attempt to ensure that changes are introduced in ways that take positive advantage of perceived external change, and that minimise any direct form of resistance to internal change. This is in the interests of the organisation. Over and beyond that, however, the organisation must attempt to remove not only any direct resistance but also the fear associated with the insecurity of the individuals within the organisation. This is especially true of structural change. Such fear has a devastating effect on morale, and morale itself has a profound effect on productivity. Ironically, the fear of change is often best minimised by ensuring that change is continual; that there is no established 'status quo' to protect.

Major change often affects the ways in which organisations are structured. Thus, a merger or major reorganisation may well break existing structures, communication channels, allegiances and so on. This is unsettling to many staff because the structure is what provides the context for their role in the organisation and a change in that structure 'devalues' that role by removing any 'stored' value associated with the old structure. One way to deal with this problem is to follow the guidance given in the human relations literature about planning for and implementing change in ways that take account of natural resistance to, and fear of, change. The most important consideration here is to keep people who will be affected by change aware of the nature and extent of proposed change. Ideally, those affected should also have some input into the change process so that they can claim some degree of ownership of the changed situation and thus will provide some commitment to making the new arrangements work.

While such guidance is undoubtedly sound, this path makes the basic mistake of attacking a symptom rather than the basic problem. This basic problem is that the very structures we use actually create the problem. The structures in the vast majority of cases, in all sectors and sizes of organisation, are extremely rigid, well defined, hierarchical and 'traditional'. They tend to result in decisions being taken 'at the top' and action taking place 'at the bottom'. Many large organisations are riddled with bureaucratic procedures that attempt to exercise control; the control of employee travel expenses is possibly the most common example. Such rigid control processes have two major disadvantages. Firstly, they can be extremely costly; often a large portion of the cost is involved in controlling a relatively small part of organisational expenditure. Secondly, they eliminate freedom of action at lower levels of the organisation. This is possibly their main aim, and yet its effect is to demotivate those who are being controlled, not only in the areas of direct control but in other areas as well. Thus a new situation which requires a decision to be taken where there is no established precedent often must be pushed up the hierarchy to the point where freedom of action is sanctioned. This can be slow and, again, costly. Indeed it may be so slow as to prevent the process from taking place at all. Those at the 'bottom end' realise that a decision will be too late to be effective and thus allow an opportunity to pass by or allow a 'mistake' to proceed. Such control structures and practices are eminently suitable for the planning and control of regular and consistent work but they were designed in a different age when the pace of change was far slower and the future was certain. In a world of uncertainty and rapid change, they prove to be inadequate.

We need structures (and perhaps we should stop using that word since it implies a degree of permanence, and start using the phrase 'working arrangements' instead) that are inherently flexible and allow change to be made easily without causing uncertainty. Instead of building a firm and permanent structure we need much more of a 'scaffolding' around which we can build temporary structures. Such structures are possible (and one possible form is discussed in Chapter 6) but require imagination – a factor lacking in much of UK management. Of course, the very introduction of any new form of working arrangement (even one designed to reduce future resistance to change) will be resisted for the reasons we have mentioned above. Thus, the change must be made with care and at a rate appropriate to the ability of the organisation, and the individuals within it, to cope with it.

Risk taking

New working arrangements are not the only thing necessary to be successful in an age of uncertainty. There is a danger that managers when faced with an uncertain future may abdicate from forward planning. This is one way of reading the results of the National Westminster Bank survey referred to above – those who did not feel sufficiently confident to read the effects of what is a well-publicised change, simply decided to wait and see. Planning must go ahead – but with a degree of flexibility to match the uncertainty of the particular planning horizon. The same flexibility must apply to those responsible for the planning and decision-making processes as to the plans themselves. The concept of the 5- or 10-year plan as practised 20 or 30 years ago has had to change. There must be much more analysis of external variables and much more contingency planning for those variables taking different values. The concept of planning and the nature of the planning process must change to reflect the nature of the type of result required. The skills required by the planners (and the managers) must change to reflect this. The same attitude of involving those who are part of the proposed change in the process of change (and the decision-making process in particular) must be extended to planning. Thus, there needs to be a combination of top-down and bottom-up approaches to planning.

Attitudes to risk must also change. Uncertainty implies risk in planning. Most managers who have some form of management training have essentially been taught to avoid risk, by planning it out of their systems. One of the major differences between 'managers' and 'businessmen' is the attitude to risk. Businessmen, besides taking an interest in a whole organisation, accept risk as inevitable. In fact some seem actively to enjoy taking risks. Of course, the sensible option is to arrange a portfolio of risks so that the overall chance of success is high but some risks that fail can be absorbed. The uncertainty associated with rapid change means that managers (especially those with responsibility for full business units) are going to have to accept risk-taking as inevitable. They should still do all in their power to minimise the risks and to balance risks, one with another, but they must adopt the philosophy that in an age of uncertainty, all is at risk. Their job is to minimise the risks and to prepare for the uncertainties.

Another key factor in addressing uncertainty is that of information provision. In fact, one definition of uncertainty is:

> the difference between the amount of information required to perform a task and the amount of information already possessed by the organisation[3].

This is slightly simplistic in that information has two attributes: quantity and quality. Thus the aim of information provision can be said to be the provision of sufficient quality information to reduce uncertainty. Two important factors are thus organisational structure and information provision. The relationship between these two factors will be further explored in Chapter 6.

One of the effects of continual change can be identified by observing the declining numbers entering some of the professional bodies. There is a much greater tendency for people now to move from role to role and from career to career rather than remaining in one particular channel and moving up it. There is a much higher demand for generalists than specialists and for experience gained in a number of roles and a number of industries. The senior managers of the future are likely to have spent their early years job hopping and industry hopping. The British Computer Society has identified the concept of the 'hybrid manager' who acquires managerial skills but also acquires information technology (IT) skills and expertise since such skills and knowledge areas continue to have a greater effect on the ways in which organisations are structured and operate. The true hybrid has a wider range of skills and abilities, gained from continually moving between functional areas, and even between organisations.

Technological change

We have already made reference to the fact that part of the change around us is obviously concerned with technological change. This is now moving faster than ever before and accelerating. This itself gives rise to a number of problems. One might consider that organisations who adopt some technological breakthrough with high speed are better faced to deal with the future, having gained some advantage over their competitors or rivals. This may be the case. However, when the investment required to adopt a major technological change is very large, the organisation may be faced with a debt on facilities that could rapidly be overtaken by the next revision of the technology. In such a case, the cautious 'tortoise' organisation could leapfrog the initial advantage gained by the 'hare'. Thus, a decision must be taken not only about whether to enter a technology race, but when to join in. On the other side of the equation is the fact that there are still people waiting to buy their first pocket calculator because, as was mentioned above, they continually see new, forthcoming models being advertised with additional features.

Many organisations must carry out technological tracking of some form, either because they are in a particular hi-tech marketplace or because they may make use of technology to provide services and functions in support of their own activity. There is also a third reason: technological change provides major market opportunities – for both product and service organisations. Earlier mention was made of the example of the growth of sales of laser printers which has led to growth in two support areas: some of those organisations that make and/or supply typewriter and computer printer ribbons have extended their range to include replacement cartridges for laser printers; and a new market has grown of organisations that will take spent cartridges and restock them at a price significantly below that of a new cartridge. Hi-tech change often creates a demand for supporting low-tech services, but equally it can destroy the demand for an existing support service. The organisation that fails to monitor technological change will at best miss out on possible opportunities, and, at worst, fail to see the threat to its own existing markets until it is too late.

The rate of external change must be matched by some internal response – a response which should not advocate change for its own sake but which must propose and implement change appropriate to meeting the changing environment. The old adage 'If it ain't broke, don't fix it' cannot apply to organisations in this age of uncertainty. Those organisations who act complacently because current performance and results appear satisfactory (or better) will be overtaken by events.

The future just happens if we let it. Our aim should be to shape it to our vision of what it should be.

Change necessitates change. Those who do not recognise this will not be part of organisations fit for the twenty-first century.

Keynotes

The past was concerned with increasing standardisation. Now we are moving into an age of increasing diversification.

The nature of change is itself becoming more unpredictable and uncertain.

Even those who may welcome change will be wary of change that comes too fast or too often.

Some organisations react to resistance to change by avoiding it. In the changing environment we have described above, this is a recipe for disaster.

The fear of change is often best minimised by ensuring that change is continual; that there is no established 'status quo' to protect.

An organisation must attempt to remove not only any direct resistance to change but also the fear associated with the insecurity of the individuals within the organisation.

The job of the management team is to minimise risks and to prepare for uncertainties.

The organisation that fails to monitor technological change will at best miss out on possible opportunities and, at worst, fail to see the threat to its own existing markets until it is too late.

Discussion topics

Identify an organisation which has suffered owing to changes in its external environment. Could the changes have been predicted? Could action have been taken to ensure that the organisation in fact benefited from, instead of suffered from, the change?

Over the next few years the Western and particularly European, economies are likely to be significantly affected by the political and economic changes taking place in Eastern Europe. What types of organisation may benefit from these changes (in the short term and in the long term)? What type of organisation may suffer? What opportunities are presented for start-up companies?

References

1 Tofler, A. (1985) *The adaptive organisation*. Aldershot: Gower.

2 *Small business and 1992: A survey*, 1992 special edition of *National Westminster Small Business Digest*.

3 Galbraith, J. (1973) *Designing complex organisations*. Wokingham: Addison-Wesley.

PART TWO

How much productivity?

Introduction

All organisations have goals. Achievement of these goals is the driving force behind organisational activity. Success is measured by the achievement of the goals. An organisation that has no goals cannot succeed; and an organisation that has no means of measuring achievement of goals is unlikely to. Not only do we need to know when a goal has been achieved; we also need to measure our progress towards goals. If productivity is included among our goals, productivity measurement becomes an important part of the management process.

In Part 1 we introduced a new concept – that of 'top-line productivity'. This Part introduces the concept of productivity and general performance measurement, and discusses how traditional measurement techniques and programmes can be extended and enhanced to measure this top-line productivity.

4 Performance and p   indicators

We have established that measurement is an important pa   ...management process (some would claim vital) but also that overconcentrᴜᴜon on measurement may lead to the neglect of factors that are not easily measured. Measurement is common for many factors and is the fundamental basis of all accounting systems. Measurement of the ability of parts of an organisation to meet the goals laid down for them is less widespread but still reasonably common. Where measurement as such is not carried out, some form of assessment must be made. Much attention has been focused on this area in the last few years and the term 'performance indicator' has come into general usage, especially in the public sector where the 'easy' alternative of measuring profitability is not available, and there is a demand for increased efficiency, which cannot be stimulated by competition.

Traditionally, performance has been associated with efficiency and has been used as a 'low-level' indicator to assess how 'hard' a person, machine or department has been working. Performance measures are thus comparable to productivity measures in that they relate an output to the inputs used to achieve that output. Generally, effectiveness has not been incorporated into measures of performance. In fact, one of the great dangers of productivity or performance measurement is that there may be a tendency to concentrate on factors which are easily and directly measurable rather than those that have a major contribution to organisational effectiveness.

One emerging problem is that there has lately been an interest shown in measuring competence of employees in work situations. This has resulted from the slow but steady trend to skills-based training and away from knowledge-based learning. Recent initiatives from the Training Agency within the UK and the National Council for Vocational Qualifications concentrate on the assessment of skills and competencies. Unfortunately, this is often described as performance assessment. In our discussions we are assuming competence; the word 'performance' relates to a quantitative assessment of level of work. See Case example 4.1.

Another area of growing interest is that of performance appraisal. This is normally aimed at assessing the performance of individuals where suitable measures are not readily available, and consists of a formalised procedure for evaluating the work performed by and perhaps attitude of an individual. This is normally carried out by the immediate superior but there may be additional processes and procedures to ensure validity and 'fair play'. Appraisal systems can be used as the basis of

---

...ple 4.1

...age mechanic carries out a service on a motor vehicle. The time given in the ...anufacturer's service manual is 2.5 hours. The mechanic takes 3 hours. This would normally give him a low performance measure. However, the job may have been carried out effectively. If the owner brings the car back after a 2-hour service for remedial work or if the car is returned for a fault that could have been detected during the service, the garage has one dissatisfied customer and a mechanic with a high performance level.

---

counselling and staff development schemes or in a more 'judgemental' role which may include pay-review and promotion-related decisions. Such appraisal systems are not essentially part of any productivity improvement process but the counselling/ development form may be useful as a contributing factor if carried out effectively. The nature of such systems leaves them outside of our discussion of performance and productivity indicators.

One interesting and important factor that must be borne in mind when selecting and implementing performance measures or indices is that 'you get what you measure'. Thus if a system for monitoring the number of times a fitter attends to a particular machine is established, the fitters will undoubtedly increase the number of times they attend to the designated machines. They will not necessarily perform effective work when attending to the machines (since this is not being monitored and evaluated), nor is this measure necessarily the best way of improving the effectiveness of the fitters. Thus, performance measures must accurately reflect the aims and intention of the organisation. What we measure must be what we need to achieve in direct support of declared objectives.

Other types of measure

Performance measures should properly relate output(s) to input(s). There may be a need for other types of measures, such as capital investment per employee, but, as in this case, these often relate one input to another and cannot be regarded as true measures of performance. The term continues to be abused, however, by being used in a very broad way which subsumes financial ratios and productivity measures. In practice, most organisations require a mix of the various types of measure, and the term 'performance indicator' offers a useful 'catch-all' phrase for describing any measure which fits into the overall framework for measuring or assessing performance. Performance indicators can thus be extremely useful, but only if their limitations are accepted.

Managers need some measure of 'performance' to serve an essential part of the management process. This process can be expressed simply as:

Goal-setting the determination of the objectives to be achieved by the organisation

40

as a whole (senior management) or by specific subunits (middle and junior management).

Planning identifying the steps and tasks that must be accomplished to meet the goals.

Organising allocating resources to carry out the required steps and activities; ensuring that appropriate structures and procedures exist to link together the resources and the manner in which they are utilised.

Monitoring measuring progress towards the goals and the resources consumed at intermediate points.

Controlling comparing monitored performance to planned performance and taking corrective action where necessary.

Separate threads run through the process of management – principally those of leadership and motivation. These threads extend throughout the entire process rather than being stages in it.

The nature and level of the particular activities within these broad categories will naturally differ, dependent on the nature of the organisation, the nature of the activity, and the nature of the individual manager. For example, lower levels of management may spend a greater proportion of their time on monitoring and controlling, whereas at senior levels more time will be devoted to goal-setting and organising. The broad shape of the process will, however, remain. The 'job' of the process is to ensure that the goals laid down in the first phase of the process are realised by the rest of the process. For some goals, achievement is obvious. For others, especially 'subgoals' used as milestones on the way to a 'greater goal', this is not the case. In such situations, measures have to be made to evaluate progress towards the goal. Performance measures meet a part of this need.

As a simple example, many organisations today categorise themselves as 'equal opportunity employers'. However, the majority of them have no way of knowing if this is true since they maintain no significant records or monitoring procedures to ensure that employment and recruitment patterns match or move towards the pattern of ethnic mix in the society in which they operate and recruit. An organisation which has a goal of being an equal opportunity employer (as distinct from one that pays lip service to the ideal) needs to institute some form of staff audit to measure the current situation and then to monitor recruitment policies and procedures to check the mix of newly employed staff. Without such 'measurement' it is difficult, if not impossible, to identify progress towards the goal. In turn, without an indication of progress being made, commitment and motivation is difficult to maintain.

Different measures will be required for different areas of activity and to satisfy the needs of different audiences. An operational manager, for example, requires measures which offer considerably more detail and which operate over a shorter timescale than a board of directors or shareholders. However, where there are several measures in use it is essential that they are related, one to another, in such a way that all are measures which contribute to the achievement of overall goals. The Pareto rule should be invoked when attempting to decide on which measures or ratios are important. The organisation must determine which of the output and input factors contribute most to overall performance; for example, is this a capital- or labour-intensive organisation? Sometimes, unfortunately, the major contributing factors may be outside the control of the organisation (e.g. the price of raw material) and thus not suitable for inclusion in performance measures. In this case, some attempt should be made to find ways of providing such control, perhaps, for example, through longer-term negotiated agreements with suppliers.

It is worth repeating that if no formal measures exist, measurement of a subjective nature will take place. Where no formal staff appraisal system is in place, supervisors will 'measure' the worth of their subordinates. Similarly those organisations who undertake a quality or customer care programme without formally measuring the results, will obtain a 'feel' for their success. This form of subjective judgement is, at best, vague and unhelpful and, at worst, counterproductive.

The very act of constructing a measurement programme is often enough to give substantial benefits, even if the resulting measures are never implemented or are flawed in some way. Although there may be conceptual or technical difficulties in arriving at and implementing suitable performance measures, the thought and discussion that goes into the process is generally very beneficial in making people attempt to identify what they should be achieving and how their success – or failure – could be measured, and the problems are rarely insurmountable.

Aims and objectives

Management by objectives (MbO) is not the fashionable management technique it once was. It has, though, left its mark on most management training courses and on a great many organisations. Most managers would talk about aims and objectives and the majority would be in agreement that the former are generally longer term and difficult to measure, whereas the latter are shorter term and suitable for measurement. Thus an organisation may have the aim of becoming 'recognised as being the best supplier of widgets to the UK market'. This is too vague to be useful in any meaningful short-term planning cycle and thus subgoals and measurable objectives would be created to allow progress towards this aim to be planned and evaluated. Such objectives may be 'to reduce the failure rate of widgets in their first year of service from 3 per cent to 2.5 per cent' or 'to increase market share within the next 12 months from 16 per cent to 18 per cent'. These are clearly measurable. However, such targets are only of use if they are accompanied by a plan which details the means of achieving them. Issuing targets in the belief that people will have to work harder to reach them can be used in the short term but is not guaranteed either to achieve the target or to maintain good relations with the workforce.

Claims are sometimes made that it is often necessary to have qualitative objectives in certain areas because of the difficulty of identifying measurable objectives or because of the costs that would be incurred by implementing a measurement programme to provide the necessary data. This may simply be a reflection of the fact that no serious attempt has been made to translate qualitative aims into quantitative objectives. The aim, for example, of 'being a byword for quality service' can, and should be translated into quantitative measures based on customer survey.

Measurement is thus a key feature of the process of management. The fundamentals of a good 'measurement regime' are:

- Measures of effective performance arise naturally out of the management process.

  Where we have to create measures as part of the fundamental planning/controlling activity, we can use them as 'interim' performance measures for a variety of purposes. Such 'natural' measures do often need to be augmented to measure progress in specific areas, perhaps because such areas are part of a special initiative or because the nature of the work involved means that 'natural' measures are not available.

- Where a ratio is used as the basis of evaluation and/or comparison, the measurement of the numerator should include all those factors, and only those factors, which are contributed by the selected components of the denominator.

  To leave out an output factor produced by an input factor which has been included would produce spurious changes in the value of the ratio whenever some change was made to that input factor. Similarly, where that unmeasured output factor was changed and caused some corresponding change in the input factor, a spurious performance or productivity change would be recorded.

- Where the performance of a particular division, department or group of staff is being measured, the factors being measured must be within the control of that particular organisational subgroup.

  Where this is not possible, the nature of any 'external' influence must be evaluated, or at least noted. If this is not done, those being evaluated will lose faith with the evaluation process and will become demotivated.

- Output should only be credited to a measure of performance where it contributes to specified goals.

  Organisations may be involved in activity that does not contribute to such goals (the most obvious example is that of producing waste or scrap product). If such output is included within a performance measure, there will be a tendency to increase it (or at least not to reduce it) since it earns credit.

- The measurement period should be consistent with the nature of 'discretionary activity'.

Where those responsible for the activity being measured make decisions which take a certain amount of time to influence the results of the activity, the measurement period must take this into account. As a simple example, if a football team employs a new manager because its recent performances have been below the expectations of the board (and the fans), the performance of the new manager cannot be judged within the first few weeks. Immediate results may be improved but this is often a short-term phenomenon. It takes a certain time before the real changes introduced, either in terms of buying or selling players, changing training methods, improving morale and motivation, etc., will have a measurable and lasting effect on the team's performances. Certain factors (such as morale) can then be measured with a degree of confidence after the initial settling-in period; others will require much longer periods before reliable and confident assessments of change may be made.

- Lower-level measurements should contribute to higher-level measurements.

If the objectives we are trying to achieve are themselves hierarchical, in that at a given level we are trying to achieve specific targets which will enable us to more readily achieve another (higher level) target, then so must our range of performance measures. When we set up a system of performance measurement, we should do so on a coherent basis across the organisation so that we can feed data obtained from performance measurement at specific levels into the measurement process at higher levels. If measurements are not constructed in this way there is a danger of suboptimisation where the productivity of a subunit is raised to the detriment of the wider organisation; for example, the productivity of a typing pool could be increased, but the service offered to the managers who use it could be lowered.

- Performance measures should not encourage a concentration on short-term results at the expense of longer-term aims.

When groups or individuals know that their performance is being measured over a set time-period, there is a natural tendency to concentrate on getting a good assessment or measurement. One sees salesmen ensuring that orders are processed to meet a particular measurement deadline. Such concentration can distort figures over a longer time and can sometimes involve considerable (wasted) effort in the manipulations required.

- Team or group measures are more effective than individual measures.

Performance measures should apply to a cohesive group of employees. Team measures are less threatening to individuals, encourage co-operation and improve team spirit.

- Teams should be involved in the determination of measures that apply to their activity.

It is important that teams or groups accept 'ownership' of the performance measures that apply to them. This is best achieved if they are involved in the discussions that lead to the formulation of the measurement process.

- Each team, or each individual if measurement is taken to that level should be contributing to a small number of key measures.

In a large, complex organisation it is perfectly feasible (though not necessarily wise) to implement a performance measurement regime involving a wide range and large number of performance indices. Any one team or individual within the organisation should not, however, be faced with concentration on more than two or three key performance measures linked to major responsibilities. A greater number will tend to distract and to dissipate effort.

- The measures of performance must produce consistent and comparable data over time.

This normally means that the criteria of measurement and the measurement process should be clear and well established so that they are and remain independent of whoever (or whatever) is carrying out the measurement.

The measures of performance should be selected so that they can be used as the basis of forward planning, prioritisation and action. See Figure 4.1.

Performance measures in higher education

Naturally it is not always possible to use measures which satisfy all of the principles shown in Figure 4.1. The problems of selecting suitable measures of performance can be illustrated by consideration of the world of higher education. Over the past few years there has been increasing pressure put on universities and polytechnics to 'increase their effectiveness'. The first problem is, of course, to define the aims of such institutions. We are all aware that their basic aim is to 'educate', but what does this really mean? Do we want them to turn out students ready for employment in the kinds of jobs we anticipate will be around three, four or more years from now? Do we expect more than a straight vocational education? If so, what more and how much of it? In the light of this fundamental difficulty of defining their aims, how do we measure their effectiveness?

Performance measures are starting to appear in such institutions and in other

---

Action plan for defining performance indicators

1 Identify a range of potential performance indicators.
2 Describe the nature of each one in terms of what it really measures and the organisational (sub)objectives it relates to.
3 Determine which indicators are readily measurable.
4 Identify those measures for which measurement data is currently available and those for which it could be provided fairly easily.
5 Determine those for which additional data must be determined.
6 Check the relationship between different indicators: the degree of overlap, mutual reinforcement, duplication, etc.
7 Identify what should be the dominant indicators and which should or could be subsidiary.
8 Clarify the degree to which each measure will help achievement of organisational goals.
9 Prioritise the list of indicators in terms of importance and in terms of ease of use.
10 Establish group workshops to discuss the range of indicators and obtain feedback on their perceived value.
11 Determine the indicators to be used.
12 Establish any additional information systems required to collect appropriate data.

Figure 4.1

public-sector organisations such as the National Health Service. A key word often used is 'accountability'; those whose capital is used to finance an undertaking should be able to judge the performance of those who act on their behalf and should be able to exercise sanctions where necessary.[1] As yet, though, the debate on the suitability of particular measures continues. The government is looking for 'efficiency' since the public purse is continually being stretched in an increasing number of directions and thus may choose the long-established measure of staff–student ratios. Although this may be regarded as a suitable efficiency measure, it makes no reference to the 'quality' of education provided.

Should we therefore look at the number and level of degrees awarded by a university? If a university awards a greater number of first and upper second-class honours degrees for the same input of resources, is it more effective? Some within higher education would argue that the quality of the output (the degrees awarded) is directly linked to the quality of the input (the nature of the students recruited). Thus, those universities or polytechnics that, for whatever reason, can attract better students have a higher potential for producing a quality output. Similarly, if the effectiveness of the secondary education sector is improved, entrants into the higher education institutions should be better prepared and the output of these higher level institutions should rise, with little or no change in the resources consumed. They would thus be recorded as having increased their productivity. These arguments suggest that to obtain a real measure of the output requires the evaluation of the quality of student at input and subsequent evaluation at output. The difference is the result of the educational process and is a 'truer' measure of the effectiveness of the institution. We are then moving towards a top-line productivity measure.

This approach is similar to the concept of 'added value' that has been used in commercial organisations as a measure of performance. In such cases, it is normally a measure of the monetary value added to inputs (raw materials, components, etc.) to produce the finished products. It does have the advantage that high-quality goods or goods with any particular form of 'customer appeal' that results in advantageous pricing, have higher added value. It can therefore be regarded as a simple means of obtaining a measure that relates to top-line productivity.

One problem with the concept of added value is that it is a 'catch-all' attribute. It is difficult to identify subcomponents of the total value added by a process. Thus, using it as a measure for anything less than the complete organisation may contravene some of the principles we have just discussed. For example, as a measure of the performance of a subgrouping of the organisation it may be invalidated by the fact that the particular subgrouping has control over only a small part of the total added value. Yet, if we only use the global measure of added value it is difficult to diagnose what is wrong (or right) when added value changes significantly. In addition, the added value measure of effectiveness normally takes no account of capital employed. Heavy capital investment will (hopefully) raise the value added but there is no indication in most standard value-added measurement schemes of this additional resource being consumed. As with all measures that operate using financial data, there is also the necessity to remove the effects of inflation from any comparative measure over different time periods. However, even with all these difficulties, added value does offer certain benefits as a measure of the wellbeing of an organisation.

In our higher education example, the concept of 'added value' emerged as a possible performance measure which may be acceptable to those involved in the process. However, the nature of the measurement (evaluating students at both input and output stages) requires measurement which does not normally exist. Thus, the measurement itself will consume resources and it can be argued that our pursuit of productivity starts by itself lowering the productivity of the institution.

Performance measures in the Health Service

Problems involved in finding suitable performance indicators are further highlighted by consideration of health services. Hospitals, in particular, are increasingly expected to be 'efficient' providers of health care. The costs associated with inpatient stay can naturally be logged. Again, however, the problem of assessing the quality of 'care' complicates any measurement of simple costs and their inclusion in performance or productivity ratios. The costs associated with a small country hospital and a large city teaching hospital are bound to be different. Is there a corresponding difference in the value of the service provided? Similarly, how do we measure the difference in the quality of care offered to mental illness patients from a hospital or a community care programme? The basic policies of care have fundamental effects on the productivity measures. If we wish to measure the productivity of the institution as a whole, we have the additional problem of coping with the 'product range' of in-patient care, out-patient facilities, teaching, research, community involvement, etc. Even restricting measurement to the fundamental element of in-patient care leaves us with a number of problems. One is the degree to which we wish to concentrate on 'process measures' or 'outcome measures'.[2] Process measures are those concerned with the operational activity of the institution. What was done? How often? At what times?

Output measures concentrate on the characteristics of the subject on which the processes are carried out and attempt to measure the outcomes. As a general rule, process measures are more appropriate as measures of inputs or measures of efficiency, and outcome measures for measures of output or measures of effectiveness. The problem of performance measurement can be, in part, illustrated by the fact that the National Health Service in the UK has changed its drive on 'performance measures' to 'Health Service measures', partly because whether performance is being measured is in some doubt and probably, partly for 'political' reasons.

Quality assurance is a parallel drive in the health care industry and it appears that this industry is now going through many of the debates and discussions that manufacturing industry went through some years ago. As manufacturing industry is responding to the debate on Quality Assurance versus Quality Management (as in TQM), the health industry is just entering the first phase. This suggests that the development is an evolutionary process – perhaps assurance of the 'traditional' kind is necessary to identify problem areas and issues and to identify baseline information before the development of 'more advanced' forms of quality management.

Process versus outcome measures
The issue of outcome versus process measures is highlighted by the common approach of an organisation attempting to measure the 'performance' of its clerical workers by logging such items as the number of invoices passed for payment, the number of telephone calls made, etc. These are process measures, and bear no relation to the fundamental aims of the organisation. They are thus dangerous to use as measures of performance. Wherever possible such measures should be replaced with 'end measures' which relate to the objectives set.

For example, a customer complaints section may deal with an average of 200 complaints per day. If the quality or availability of the goods or services provided declines over time, the number of complaints may rise. If the customer complaints section handles this increasing number of complaints without a corresponding increase in resources, their productivity as measured by complaints handled per member of staff will obviously rise. Yet, we would hardly use this as a measure of increasing effectiveness of the organisation. This is an indication of the type of 'sub-optimisation' referred to above. The objective must be to reduce the number of complaints and even if we accept that, in the short term, it is impossible to reduce the number to zero, then a more useful measure of the effectiveness of this section would be linked to the satisfaction of complaining customers with the way in which their complaint was handled and addressed. Similarly, an effective maintenance section might be extremely inefficient in that ideally, they should have little work to do. Measuring and improving their efficiency, by number of faults attended and corrected, is not the way to make the organisation as a whole more effective.

The current emphasis on process rather than outcome measures can be further exemplified by the traditional job description or job specification. An actual job description for a computing support officer for a CAD/CAM facility listed responsibilities as:

1 Create and maintain a register of authorised users and account information.

2 Back-up both system software and user files regularly.

3 Provide systems support to users.

4 Assist in the installation of third-party software.

5 Monitor and report on network performance.

6 Maintain and update system programs.

All these are process-related tasks. They do not tell us what the system and/or users should be able to do.

Changing to an output-oriented viewpoint is not easy. Generally, when an organisation is asked to revise its view and to start writing job descriptions and other documentation with output-related tasks and activities, the number of items in such a list is significantly reduced. This is a good sign. In terms of outcomes, most jobs have a small number of measurable outcomes which actively support the objectives of their department and the enterprise. Any addition to this list simply detracts from the key or core activities of the job.

In the above example, some of the process-related activities will convert naturally to output (or outcome) measures. The first entry in the list could be rewritten as:

1 Reduce to zero the number of attempts to log-on to the system by unauthorised users.

This naturally leads to a measure of effectiveness of the selected output or outcome measure. This process of separating process from outcome is similar to the carrying out of the EXAMINE stage of the basic method study procedure – see Chapter 8. In simplistic terms this involves the asking of a set of predetermined questions about a problem or situation that needs to be resolved or changed. The first set of questions, known as the primary questions are:

- WHAT is achieved?

- WHY is it necessary?

- WHO does it?
- WHERE is it done?
- WHEN is it done?
- HOW is it done?

Further questions are used to elicit alternative suggestions and to arrive at a changed situation.

When these questions are asked there is a tendency to confuse the WHAT and the HOW (in effect, to confuse the outcome with the process). Thus, in a simple packing line, the final stage might be to wrap string around a parcel to secure it ready for transport. Inexperienced method study practitioners are likely, in response to the question 'WHAT is achieved?' to answer 'The parcel is tied with string'. This answer is the HOW and answering like this at this stage affects – in a negative way – the answers to all of the other questions. The correct answer to this question is 'The parcel is secured'; the fact that it is tied with string is the answer to the question HOW?

It is important that outcome and process are separated and that we continue to ask, especially, WHAT and WHY before HOW. If we can change the answers to the first two, the third becomes a redundant question.

Future strategy measures

The importance of selecting measures to be used as the basis of future planning and action can also be demonstrated by returning to our consideration of customer complaints handling. Naturally most organisations should be looking at ways of removing the causes of customer complaints. If, however, we think of the types of dissatisfied customers we have, they can be categorised as:

Dissatisfied customers who *make no complaint* to us but spread a message of dissatisfaction among other customers and potential customers. This 'word-of-mouth' non-recommendation can be very damaging.

Dissatisfied customers who *complain to us*. Such customers may have their complaints handled in such a way that either satisfies them and persuades them to give us repeat business or dissatisfies them and causes them to end their association with our organisation.

Should we concentrate on ensuring that we have no dissatisfied customers by addressing our standards of quality and service? Or should we concentrate on improving our complaints handling to ensure that complaining customers end up sufficiently satisfied to give us their repeat business?

The answer is, naturally, both. But the nature of our product/service range and the proportion of our customers who fall into the above categories may well affect

the proportion of our resources (in the short and long terms) that we assign to
of the 'solutions'. Before we can carry out this process, we need reliable information
performance measures of customer satisfaction. We may be dealing with relatively
'soft' information here but it should be possible to make some estimate, based on
surveys of customers, as to the proportions of satisfied and dissatisfied customers,
the proportions of complaining customers who end up satisfied and dissatisfied, the
proportion of our business which is repeat business from each category, and so on.

One of the problems with good quality and service is that it can be too unobtru-
sive. Customers who never have need to complain will not have bad feelings about
our organisation, but they may never get strong good feelings. A customer who
complains and is handled well may actually feel more strongly about the good
quality of service than those who had no cause for complaint. Again, a properly
constructed customer survey may provide information that allows us to judge such
issues. Armed with such information we can start to make rational decisions of our
future service strategy.

One starting point for determining performance and productivity areas is to
determine the key areas of any job that should be influenced by the measurement
process. For a production supervisor, these may be:

- production quantity;
- production quality;
- production cost;
- health and safety of workers;
- work-in-progress.

Thus, performance or productivity measures which include or address such factors,
perhaps by linking them together, should be established. Under some circumstances,
particularly for coherent low-level jobs where weightings can be attached to each of
the factors, it may be possible to establish one measure (a multifactor measure)
which takes into account all of the appropriate factors.

Again, a helpful approach is to examine each of these areas and to list the inputs,
the processes and the outputs of each one. Productivity measures can be constructed
from examination of the outputs and the related or corresponding inputs.

Limitations in performance measures can be more readily accepted when the
measures are to be used for comparative purposes only (and not as any 'absolute'
measure) and when a degree of variability is accepted. When measuring the performance of hospitals, for example, the large number being measured allows the establishment of a mean or median performance on a given measure. The majority of
hospitals will be grouped reasonably closely around this point, and attention and
concern can be focused on those hospitals which lie outside of this acceptable

nciple can be applied to a company with a large number of work

ng on a similar task or range of tasks.

paragraphs highlight both the importance of selecting appropri-

ome of the difficulties in establishing performance measures

ul and perceived to be 'fair'. Those which are not perceived as

tivators and must therefore be avoided.

...shed that monitoring and control must be moved down from the level of the organisation (where measures are too aggregated to be used to provide the specific information needed) to attack local areas of interest. Should we then carry on until we start to measure individual performance and productivity?

Performance evaluation

Within the field of work study, there is a more specific use of the word 'performance' to describe an evaluation of the rate of working of an operator over a shift or day. In order to understand the concept of 'standard performance'[3], we must first understand the concept of the 'average, qualified worker' since standard performance describes the rate at which this mythical worker will work. Thus when times for jobs are issued after work measurement, they are issued for this average, qualified worker. Similar uses of 'average' people are used in many other areas. The problem is that people are not average. By definition, many must be above average and many must be below it. People have different physical attributes, attitudes, skills, needs, and so on and are thus unlikely to work at the same pace. The concept of the average worker is a valid one for aggregating times or performances as the basis of planning, but it is open to question as the basis of individual measurement for appraisal or payment-by-results systems. Automatically branding a significant portion of the workforce as 'below average' may create ill feeling.

In most fields of work, within all sectors of industry and commerce, the performance of an organisation is dictated by the way in which the 'system' works (the way in which the organisation is structured, managed and administered) and by the way in which the people work. Problems and errors may be system errors or people errors. In most organisations, and especially larger ones, the majority of performance and error is dictated by the system with the workforce contributing a minor role. Thus, to concentrate on the performance of individuals is often unproductive. We should accept that people are different. We should allow a margin for those differences and only be aroused when the performance of an individual or group falls outside of our allowed range. We should then concentrate on raising the performance of the overall system. Performance and productivity measurement is therefore best carried out on 'natural' subgroupings of the organisation; to take it down to the level of the individual may be counterproductive.

Further problems are created when such measures are used as the basis of payment-by-results schemes. Where the work of an individual or small group is measured and used as the basis of their payment, say by offering a bonus for work done in excess of an agreed standard level, those individuals or groups naturally feel aggrieved if they are prevented from increasing their output by system inefficiencies. A common occurrence is that one group of employees spends time waiting because components have not been delivered from an earlier stage in the process. Often, some form of compensation is given to recognise the fact that a reduction from the average performance of the individual or group (which would result in a fall from the average earnings level) is not the 'fault' of those receiving the payment. This compensation may take the form of a credit of work to compensate for the lost opportunity. This credit enables the calculation of performance, on which the calculation of bonus payment is made, to move, at least some way, towards the figure it would have been if the individual or group had not been prevented from working at its chosen rate. The performance as measured is now false. A number of occurrences of this form of compensation can result in a measurement regime giving adequate reward to employees but inaccurate and unreliable information to management.

In all organisations given careful thought and proper discussion it must be possible to determine effective measures of performance and to prevent the kinds of distortion we have just discussed. The advantages of establishing a systematic measurement regime are that it avoids the totally subjective, and often erroneous, judgements that are bound to take place in the absence of formally constituted measures and that because it is designed to be comprehensive, it should avoid the problems of suboptimisation that come from a partial system implemented to serve one particular aim (wage payment, for example), rather than being designed as part of an overall productivity measurement and improvement programme.

Keynotes

One of the great dangers of productivity or performance measurement is that there may be a tendency to concentrate on factors which are easily and directly measurable rather than those that make a major contribution to organisational effectiveness.

For some goals, achievement is obvious. For others, especially 'subgoals' used as milestones on the way to a 'greater goal', this is not the case. In such situations, measures have to be made to evaluate progress towards the goal.

Measurement is a key feature of the process of management.

Those whose capital is used to finance an undertaking should be able to judge the performance of those who act on their behalf and should be able to exercise sanctions where necessary.

Wherever possible 'process' measures should be replaced with 'end measures' which relate to the objectives set.

Performance measures which are not perceived as fair will act as demotivators and must therefore be avoided.

The concept of the average worker is a valid one for aggregating times or performances as the basis of planning, but it is open to question as the basis of individual measurement for appraisal or payment-by-results systems.

The advantages of establishing a systematic measurement regime are that it avoids the totally subjective, and often erroneous, judgements that are bound to take place in the absence of formally constituted measures; and that because it is designed to be comprehensive, it should avoid the problems of suboptimisation that come from a partial system implemented to serve one particular aim (wage payment, for example), rather than being designed as part of an overall productivity measurement and improvement programme.

Discussion topics

Obtain a job description from within your own organisation. Identify those entries which relate to process and those which relate to outcome. Rewrite those entries that are process-related so that they become output-related. Can any of these entries be omitted from the job description without significantly affecting the measure of effectiveness of the work being carried out?

You are, once again, a theatre manager. What kinds of measures would you use to indicate that you were running an effective operation? How would you collect the data to make up the measures?

Have you ever made a complaint to a supplier about a product/service? What was it? Was it dealt with to your satisfaction? Have you used that supplier since?

References

1 Smith, P. 'The use of performance indicators in the public sector', *Journal of the Royal Statistical Society*, A (1990) **153** Part 1, pp. 43–72.

2 *Measurement and interpretation of productivity* (1979). Washington, DC: National Academy of Sciences.

3 *Glossary of terms used in management services* (1992). London: British Standards Institution.

5 A top-line productivity measurement programme

The previous chapter leads us to the inescapable fact that there is no single off-the-shelf measurement regime that can be applied to all organisations. Measures must be constructed to satisfy the distinct needs of each organisation. Similarly there is no real concept of 'proper' and 'improper' measures. We have already established some guidelines for measures but the overall consideration is that we can identify and measure progress towards the objectives laid down in our corporate strategy and plan.

The productivity and performance review

Before embarking on a top-line productivity measurement (or improvement) programme, it is useful to obtain a clear picture of where the organisation currently stands with regard to productivity or performance measurement and assessment by carrying out a productivity and performance review (PPR). In the same way that productivity and performance indices are measured from a base point, this review offers a base for comparative purposes and avoids 'reinventing the wheel' where suitable measures or approaches are already in existence. A PPR thus attempts to define the range and nature of any current measures used to assess and evaluate productivity or performance within parts of or the whole of the organisation. Some measures will inevitably exist; often they will be purely financial ones concerned with the measures that are required to satisfy legislative or other external requirements (e.g. those of the Companies Act, shareholders, community charge payers or whatever).

The review may be a relatively simple questionnaire distributed to senior and middle managers and may contain questions such as those below.

- What measures are currently used to assess productivity or performance?

- Are these individual or group measures?

- How are the results used?

- What measures have previously been used and discarded?

- Are any payment or reward systems based on performance measurement?

- Are any employees responsible for measuring their own performance?

- Are current measures:

valid?

Do they measure or reflect real changes in productivity? This means, in effect, assessing whether they include the appropriate and relevant factors. For example, if a mix of outputs (of goods and/or services) is included in the measurement process, simple unit output measures are often invalid since they are comparing like with unlike. It may be necessary to convert the outputs to a common currency (such as standard hours) to enable the mix to be evaluated properly.

complete?

Do the measures contain all appropriate factors? For example, if measures are based on direct labour only, any change in the balance between direct and indirect labour may produce spurious productivity or performance changes.

comparable?

Are external influences such as price and cost changes excluded from the measure or taken account of within the measure?

timely?

Are results produced within a timescale that permits effective use to be made of the data?

targeted?

Are results distributed to and in a suitable form for the manager(s) who can make best use of them?

cost-effective?

Do the benefits accruing from the data obtained from the measurement programme justify the cost of the measurement regime?

Where no 'formal' measures are identified, managers should be asked whether they determine the effectiveness of their part of the organisation and, if so, how. If they say 'No', further questions should be asked!

This review may require a briefing meeting and individual discussions with managers to ensure that all measures are included. Thus it may be necessary to assign someone to co-ordinate the activity and consolidate results. Where the review is part of a fuller commitment to a top-line productivity programme, this can be achieved by appointing the productivity co-ordinator (see Chapter 14) before the review commences.

The next stage is to review these measures and identify which of them are being used, or are capable of being used, to change performance to offer more effective progress towards organisational goals. An attempt should therefore be made to 'allocate' each of the measures to a specific, declared objective or aim. This linking may be indirect, since some measures will be at 'low' levels, feeding into higher-level measures which can be directly linked with specific aims. This process should enable those goals to be identified which have no, or insufficient or inadequate, measures contributing to their achievement. It may also help to identify areas which are being overmeasured. This can be as big a problem as having no measures at all, since considerable effort may be going into recording data and constructing measures which have little effect since they are duplicated or overlapped elsewhere; similarly, effort may be going into manipulating results to make the measures look good.

Such a review should be promoted and seen as part of the awareness raising and training programme necessary to start the implementation of a productivity improvement programme. Thus it must be carried out in a positive manner (effective measurement assists managers in the management process) and not seen to have pejorative connotations. One approach is to hold an initial (briefing) seminar about productivity and performance measurement and improvement and then to use the questionnaire as a means of maintaining interest and allowing those involved to think more about the subject within their own organisational boundaries. It is then possible to hold a second seminar, or to publish a report, to disseminate the findings of the questionnaire and to highlight areas that require attention and/or examples of good practice. This second seminar can also be used as the starting point for 'filling in the gaps' where adequate measurement or assessment does not take place. This must be done by identifying what has to be measured and compared to assess progress towards corporate aims. Such measures are normally in two parts – outputs and inputs. Thus we need to ask:

1 What outputs do we need to measure (for the organisation or for specific subunits of it) to assess such progress?
2 What inputs go to provide such outputs?

It is worth pointing out that not all factors which contribute to productivity – especially top-line productivity – can be measured in 'hard' terms. One important factor, for example, is that of employee morale (and motivation). It may therefore be necessary to supplement any hard, quantitative measures with measures of these soft factors. This can be achieved through the use of such devices as attitude surveys, and comparative surveys at different times can measure the improvement – or worsening – of this important attribute. One such survey, to establish the base measure, is a useful part of a PPR.

At this stage, the practicability of measurement should not be a factor in the discussions. Such problems can be addressed later; the aim here is simply to establish a conceptual framework for measurement and evaluation of productivity and performance; a framework which links into the corporate aims and objectives. The measures of output and input can then be compared with currently available measures, or existing data, to establish which measures are immediately available and which require some further discussion and action.

Training

Some training may need to be given either within or in addition to the above seminars to allow managers, and others, to understand the principles of productivity and performance measurement and to inform their discussions. Such discussions may lead to some of the possible measures being eliminated as being unnecessary or invalid; the aim is to arrive at a relatively small number of key measures. If possible, once these key measures have been determined, a set of ratios or indices should be constructed from historical data, preferably over more than one measurement period so that changes can be observed and compared. The results of this 'simulation' of a measurement process can be presented to the management team to see how they compare to the established perceptions and value judgements of those involved. Either the measures or those perceptions may be changed as a result of such an exercise.

In this way, the group of managers involved can feel a degree of ownership of what eventually emerges in any revised measurement regime. It is likely that even after training these managers will need help from experienced practitioners or external consultants, but this process must be seen as a partnership with the managers whose responsibilities lie within the scope of the measurement programme.

Productivity and performance measures must be used with care. Like other measures, they can be misinterpreted. The heart of a top-line productivity improvement programme lies in the approach taken and not in the quantitative assessment of productivity. Measures, as we have seen, are useful, however, in measuring progress and in maintaining motivation.

Motivation

Sometimes 'measures' are used to motivate staff and to explain or clarify concepts. For example, in customer care it is sometimes difficult to convince some members of an organisation of the benefits that will accrue from a policy of improving customer care and customer satisfaction. However, it is possible to construct measures of customer satisfaction and to link these with lost opportunities. See Case example 5.1.

The measures used were in fact pure estimates from the managing director. (Some of them could have been established with a greater degree of reliability by surveying customers, but this would have incurred substantial cost.) However, they did serve to illustrate his point and motivate depot managers to take more seriously the issue of customer satisfaction.

Case example 5.1

Tri-Hire hires out DIY and gardening equipment from a number of 'retail' outlets. Its average hire transaction is £17.50. Customers complain (not always to Tri-Hire) when the equipment they want is unavailable, dirty, damaged or when it fails to perform to their expectations. The Managing Director constructed the following analysis and sent it to each depot manager.

Average number of complaints received per depot per week = 40 (A).

Number of complainants whose complaint is handled satisfactorily and who will return for further hire = 20 (B).

Estimated number of dissatisfied customers who do not complain = 15 (C).

Estimated average number of negative word-of-mouth contacts of each dissatisfied customer = 5 (D).

$$\text{Potential lost revenue} = ((A-B) + C) \times D \times £17.50$$
$$= £3062.50$$

Case example 5.1 also serves to reinforce the point that measures should be selected to encourage improvement in those areas of the business that are identified as the key areas – within the corporate mission and objectives.

Defining suitable measures

It is not possible to be prescriptive in defining suitable productivity or performance measures. The design of measures appropriate to a particular organisation must be a tailored approach, dependent on the nature of the organisation, its activity and its environment. It is possible, though, to offer guidance on the general approach and principles to be followed. This must then be used to build measures which will enable the particular organisation to develop measures and a measurement regime which will allow base measures to be set, and for subsequent measures to identify areas of effective improvement and good practice, while remaining aware of and allowing for the imperfections of the measures themselves.

If we go back to the basic concept of a ratio of outputs to inputs, then before deciding on suitable measures we should first clarify the 'rules of the game'. These rules include the basic principles of a measurement regime outlined in the previous chapter and, additionally, the important factor that to maintain consistency we should ideally use dimensionless ratios; the units of the numerator and denominator of the ratio should be the same. This is why money is often chosen, since many of the factors can be expressed in monetary values. However, monetary values are affected by pricing strategies (our own and those of our suppliers). Thus, if the price of electricity were to rise, any measure which related to energy usage would automatically be worsened even though our energy efficiency may have remained the same or even improved. Care must therefore be taken in deciding what exactly it is that we wish to measure, and our productivity measures may have to include a mechanism for including or identifying the effects of such price changes, perhaps by being expressed at prices in a given base year. This is a major reason why productivity measures are needed as an alternative measure to profitability. One approach is to take items within the accounting system (e.g. from the nominal ledger) and to identify them, with regard to price, as:

Controllable by our organisation   C
Uncontrollable   UC
Partially controllable   PC

The partially controllable items can be further subdivided into C and UC components or proportions.

For UC items, we need to establish a base price to be used in our measures; for others we can use actual price since, because it is under our control, it is a measure of our effectiveness in being able to sustain that price by the nature of the product or service we offer. Such classifications are often carried out as part of the normal accounting practice and should not create substantial problems for most organisations.

Particular problems arise, when using monetary measures, with the treatment of overheads. Overhead costs may be a significant part of overall costs and yet are often treated in some fairly arbitrary fashion. One common approach in many costing systems is to allocate a major share of overheads in line with labour costs. Yet, labour costs in many organisations are declining as a percentage of total costs and the logic in assigning overheads to products on a labour cost basis is not totally clear. In many industries even those overheads directly associated with products may be incurred largely before any product is made (e.g. through design and R&D expenditure).

Should such costs be attributed to products being currently manufactured or to the product they were incurred against when it comes onstream? How should they be apportioned? Activity-based costing is an alternative form of costing which allows a more logical allocation of overhead costs to products. It does this by identifying 'cost drivers', which are factors in the process of manufacture which relate to product volume and which can be associated with overhead costs. Thus, overhead items such as machine depreciation and maintenance costs can be related to the cost driver of machine hours and the relative use of products of machine time can be used as the basis of apportioning such costs. Similarly, the overhead costs of the personnel department could be related to the cost driver of labour hours.

This book is not the place for a full description of activity-based costing but such an approach does serve to offer a more rational basis for overhead allocation and ensures that performance measures based on monetary units derived from a costing system more accurately reflect the 'true' situation. Decisions then taken as a result should be more effective in helping to achieve aims and objectives.

Once we have our costing classification we can start to construct productivity or performance ratios. The examples are chosen to offer guidance on the type of measure that can be used and ways in which it may be created from available data. These measures are not top-line measures since, as yet, they take no account of top-line factors in the measurement of output. However, we shall explain the process of productivity measurement and then expand such measures to reflect the concept of top-line productivity.

One of the major classifications of spending is into revenue and capital. A basic breakdown of productivity to take this into account could be between revenue and capital productivity – the degree to which our output varied in relation to the amounts of revenue and capital that we spend. Thus, we can start our measurement regime by constructing revenue and capital productivity indices in the following manner.

Revenue productivity index
Base year: Base revenue productivity ratio (BRPR)

$$= \frac{\text{Actual delivered product/service value}}{\text{Resources consumed at actual cost}} \times 100$$

Subsequent (e.g. current) year: Current revenue productivity ratio (CRPR)

$$= \frac{\text{Delivered product/service at adjusted value}}{\text{Resource usage at adjusted cost levels}} \times 100$$

The revenue productivity index (RPI) is then:

$$= \frac{\text{CRPR}}{\text{BRPR}} \times 100$$

There is naturally a difficulty with products or services created after the establishment of a base year. Here, it is necessary either to start a new base year or to extrapolate price changes for new materials and the new products/services to the established base.

This process will still give imperfect results. However, such an index of productivity is useful for comparative purposes and to serve as the basis of discussion and productivity improvement.

Capital productivity index
The figures for output are calculated as before. The calculation of the denominator, however, depends to a degree on accounting practices within the organisation. A simple definition of capital is total assets minus current liabilities, but organisations may have their own convention. The specific components of this 'capital' must be

identified and a base value established. How this is done depends on the nature of the component and the environment and conventions of the organisation, but the task should be possible. Similar ratios to those for revenue productivity can then be calculated.

Base year: Base capital productivity ratio (BCPR)

$$= \frac{\text{Actual delivered product/service value}}{\text{Net capital worth}} \times 100$$

Subsequent (e.g. current) years: Current capital productivity ratio (CCPR)

$$= \frac{\text{Delivered product/service at adjusted value}}{\text{Adjusted net capital worth}} \times 100$$

Capital productivity index (CPI) is then:

$$= \frac{\text{CCPR}}{\text{BCPR}} \times 100$$

This index can be distorted by the expenditure on capital which takes a significant time to commission. It may be necessary in such situations to remove such capital from the ratio, and also to remove the value of product/service associated with that expenditure.

Similar ratios and indices can be established for other items/factors if required and a multifactor productivity index (MFPI) constructed such as:

Revenue and capital productivity index:

$$= \frac{(\text{RPI} \times \text{AV}) + (\text{CPI} \times \text{AW})}{\text{AV} + \text{AW}}$$

where   AV = adjusted value of goods/services;
and   AW = adjusted capital worth in the current year.

Incorporation of top-line factors

The ratios and indices described so far are based on a numerator which consists essentially of output alone – though since it is expressed in monetary terms, it does relate to other factors which govern the price we can charge, and this in turn is dependent on the top-line factors referred to in Chapter 2. We still need, however, a more effective way of incorporating top-line factors into our productivity measures.

This obviously depends on the nature of the top-line factors that we identify as important to our organisation (because they are important to our customers or clients). Some of these may be directly measurable through some relatively simple testing process. For example, reliability of manufactured goods may be evaluated through 'soak testing' routines; speed of service in a service-based organisation may be measurable through some kind of monitoring regime or by conducting sampling studies at intervals. Those that are less easily measured – such as fashionability, aesthetics and other similar factors – must be measured in other ways. The point has been made earlier that 'measures' are made by our customers in their purchasing decisions and it must, therefore, be possible for us to make some attempt at measuring. Where the factor, like those mentioned above, is evaluated subjectively by the end-user of the goods or service, we may need to conduct consumer testing of the form often carried out by marketing departments before new product/service launches. The cost of such assessments may at first seem high, but there is no substitute for knowing how customers (and potential and 'lost' customers) view our offering. As an example, British Airways, as part of its Customer First programme, interviews about 150,000 passengers per year.

With a little ingenuity it should be possible to create suitable measures for the criteria identified as having the major impact on the purchasing decisions of our customers. We then need to use these to modify our standard throughput-only productivity measures.

If we take an organisation producing a single product as an example, this could be done in the following way.

- *Identify the criteria that result in perceived value to the customer.*

This may need some form of customer research programme (information may already be available as part of market research activity). It is important to realise that it is almost essential to include competitive offerings in such an investigation since the negative factors attributed to your products may only be identified in comparison to positive factors associated with a competitor's range. Although such a study could be relatively costly, information on customers' views on your product(s) is never wasted if it is treated with respect and used to improve the offering.

Let us assume, for simplicity sake, that such an investigation identifies the prime criteria as being functionality, reliability and aesthetics.

- *Identify the relative weighting to be assigned to each of these criteria.*

These weightings should arise from the same investigation. Again, let us assume that we are using a simple numerical judgement based on customers' views that assigns values of:

Functionality   5
Reliability   3
Aesthetics   2

- *Identify suitable base or current measures for each of the criteria.*

For functionality, this could be a simple scoring system that assigns values to each of the components of function. Alternatively, a score could be obtained from the same customer investigation that identified the criteria themselves. The precise nature of the measurement is not too important since it is only to be used for comparative purposes in subsequent time periods. For aesthetics, there would have to be a subjective judgement obtained from a customer investigation. For reliability, it should be possible to obtain some quantitative measure from a testing procedure.

Again, for simplicity of explaining the methodology, let us assume that measures are obtained as follows:

Functionality 70 out of a 'perfect' 100. (The perfect score may represent some idealised concept or it could be based on the best perceived competitive offering.)

Reliability Mean time between failure: 62 hours.

Aesthetics 60 out of a 'perfect' 100 (or compared to the perceived 'best' on the market).

These become the base 'scores'.

- *Determine the proportion of 'total output' which should be carried by throughput and by these other factors.*

This is a more difficult exercise and will depend on the nature of the product, the marketplace and the particular manufacturing process. It is likely that most organisations will naturally allow only a small proportion of 'output' to be determined by such top-line factors, especially in the early months/years of such an approach. However, it should be shown that such factors are important and are being taken account of in the measure of productivity. With increased experience – and hindsight – it may be necessary to adjust these proportions in the future.

Our assumption here is that the proportion allotted to throughput is 70 per cent and to top-line factors is 30 per cent.

In any subsequent measurement period it is then necessary to repeat the investigation (or the market research) that gives the scores for each of the criterion.

Let us assume that in the year following the base year:

Functionality score = 80
Reliability = 66 hours
Aesthetics score = 60 (no change)

It is possible that subjective scores for such factors as functionality and aesthetics may change even though no changes have been made to the product, since the perception of customers may change relative to competitors' offerings. The decision not to make product changes may be conscious or subconscious, but in either case, the revised scores should be used as they determine the perception of value in the mind of the customer.

- *Calculate indices for each criterion*

    Thus, using the above figures:

    Functionality index $= \dfrac{80 \times 100}{70} = 114.3$

    Reliability index $= \dfrac{66 \times 100}{62} = 106.5$

    Aesthetics index $= \dfrac{60 \times 100}{60} = 100$

These figures are extremely useful in their own right as they indicate customer (dis)satisfaction with particular attributes of the product and they can thus be used as the basis for further investigation into the nature of the product and areas for possible improvement. They can also be used to modify any previously calculated multifactor productivity index.

- *Calculate a top-line productivity index*

    This is done by modifying the multifactor productivity index which was calculated using throughput only as the output figure, using the criterion indices and the established weighting factors for each criterion.

    Assuming the current multifactor productivity index (see above for details of calculation) is 102, then top-line factors are to account for 30 per cent of the top-line productivity index (TPI) (previously established).

    Weightings of the top-line factors are:

Functionality   5
Reliability   3
Aesthetics   2

Total weighting points = 10

Therefore, percentage of top-line index devoted to:

$$\text{Functionality} = \frac{5}{10} \times 30\% = 15\%$$

$$\text{Reliability} = \frac{3}{10} \times 30\% = 9\%$$

$$\text{Aesthetics} = \frac{2}{10} \times 30\% = 6\%$$

Then TPI = $(102 \times 70\%) + (114.3 \times 15\%) + (106.5 \times 9\%) + (100 \times 6\%)$
= 104.13

This 'final' top-line productivity index is not very different from the multifactor index calculated on the basis of throughput alone but its calculation serves two main purposes – it ensures that the index includes important factors which directly affect customer perceptions of value, and its calculation allows the creation of the subsidiary indices of each of the designated criteria. Naturally, where an organisation devotes a higher proportion of its overall productivity index to top-line factors (for example, for a company in a fashion-related industry, a very significant proportion of the index may be assigned to customer-derived factors) the index will more strongly reflect changes in such factors. Even where the difference between a throughput-only and a top-line index is small, it is worth remembering that very small changes in productivity, service and customer satisfaction levels can have a major effect on market penetration and profitability. It does, in this case, show that we are doing 'better' than our simple output figures show in that our revised figure is 104.13 compared to 102, and this is brought about by improvements (real or perceived) to our products. (This could be used by the marketing department as evidence of the fact that we should be able to increase our prices but still retain our customers.)

Targeting

Once the organisation has established a measurement regime, it should consider the setting of targets for future performance. This may be easier for subfactors or local measures, but since these feed into the larger, global measures this is not necessarily a disadvantage. If all the low-order targets are set, the target for the global measures can be constructed.

The example cited above of Tri-Hire (Case example 5.1) raises the prospect of including 'lost' or 'potential' revenues into the target revenue productivity index (RPI). Thus, if after surveying customer perceptions and complaints we can establish that there is additional potential revenue of 6 per cent, we can include some of that revenue (assuming that we will not reach perfection immediately) in our target figure. We then end up with an increased target and also target measures for the indices that will contribute to this high-level measure – we would set targets for the incidence of customer complaints, for the proportion of complaining customers who are treated sufficiently well for us not to lose their business and so on.

The measures we have discussed so far are global measures in that they attempt to measure the performance and productivity of the whole organisation. They are also essentially longer-term indicators since they cannot be used to reflect short-term changes. They serve as useful year-end (or accounting period end) measures to indicate the wellbeing of the organisation and thus may be presented to boards of directors, shareholders and other groups with long-term interests. It is still, however, necessary to derive suitable short-term measures which can more accurately reflect mid-term changes. Working from the global measures above it may be possible to derive submeasures which are constituted of the same basic output and input factors where these are directly controllable by a particular department, section or team which is being measured. Such measures are very useful in that it is easy to see the relationship between the subunit measure and the global measure. In some cases it is not possible to use the same kinds of measure. In these instances an alternative performance or productivity measure should be found – and a measure which reflects the organisation's concern for top-line factors. There may be two types of measure required at lower levels:

Managerial measures
These are measures derived from the global measures and used by the management team to assess the performance of a subunit of the organisation.

Employee measures
It is essential that employees are provided with means of enabling them to assess their own performance; such performance measures should be easily understood by those being assessed and for this reason it may not be appropriate to use ratio-derived criteria. These criteria may thus not be true performance measures (in that they may not relate an output to an input) but they must reflect the contribution of the section or group to overall objectives.

The *managerial measures* are most likely to be ratios similar in fashion to the global measures, and in fact, possible subsets of these global measures. For example, it is often possible to have a revenue productivity index calculated for each operating division or product area of an organisation where the output and input factors used within the calculation are those directly attributable to the particular division or department. There may be problems in assigning input factors where they are common to more than one area, but this can normally be done on the basis of some 'overhead' allocation.

Other measures may be single-factor measures (e.g. of labour) intended to analyse a global measure in more detail in terms of particular resource categories or account headings (e.g. training).

As an example, the sales department of an organisation will almost certainly be interested in the overall profitability or productivity of the organisation; but in addition, if it requires to examine the effectiveness of its sales force within different markets, it may require a further breakdown which shows the profitability (or value added) for each type of salesman (assuming for example that it has salesmen operating in industrial and commercial markets). A hierarchy of measures can be created starting from the global measure of output (revenue) assigned across the full sales force and showing the contribution to this of each type of salesman. One effective way of achieving such a hierarchy is to take the factors that form a given ratio and to derive subratios which together – by multiplication or division – will produce that ratio. In such a way, data collected at lower levels form the data needed at higher levels. Thus, for example, our marketing department may use ratios such as that shown in Figure 5.1.

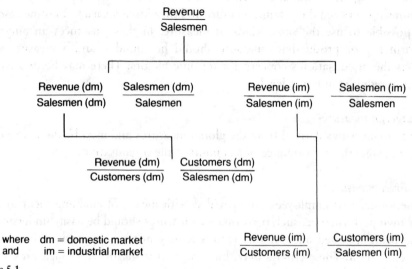

Figure 5.1

These measures – although many of them are not true performance indicators – serve to indicate resources (of salesmen) consumed in the different markets and the relative contribution of each market to total revenue. Similar measures can be constructed for different areas of activity and resource consumption.

Employee measures, as has been stated, must be meaningful to the group of employees concerned and must be easily understandable by them. This can be done by establishing a process of measurement and then converting the result onto a simple linear scale or to a suitable performance band. The first step is to decide on the criteria of effective performance for the group: this is often essentially a measure of output but should, wherever possible, be modified to take into account relevant top-line factors, where these are under the control of the group. The most obvious example is that of quality. Output itself may have to be measured in something other than units of product where the group is not responsible for a clearly defined end-product which itself relates to the end-product of the organisation. A common alternative is to make use of a 'work content' measure such as standard hours arrived at by some form of work measurement. The inclusion of top-line factors can be achieved in similar fashion to that of the global productivity measure. Consider the following example.

A group of 10 workers is responsible for producing a part of a product. The managers of the group have determined that quality of this part is very important since it has a major impact on the quality of the final product. The process being used to produce the parts involves the members of the group working very much as a team and thus absences from work have a significant detrimental effect on performance. (Although replacement workers can be drafted in, these will naturally not be trained and experienced to the same degree.) Finally, the organisation has over the last few years paid particular attention (for both 'legal' and perhaps more proper reasons) to improving its safety record. Thus the management of the section involved have had discussions with the group and agreed that any performance measure should include some assessment of:

- output;
- quality;
- absenteeism;
- safety.

Further discussions based on management priorities have resulted in a percentage weighting being assigned to these factors of:

- output 50
- quality 25
- absenteeism 15
- safety 10

The measurement period has been set at four weeks since it was felt that weekly measurement would be overprecise and destabilising.

The productivity support team has established a simple banded scale for each factor such as that for output (Table 5.1). Notice that the bands are not regular. This is because the management wished to offer smaller gaps between the higher bands to give a greater motivation to achieve the next band and the additional point on the scale. On each scale, a score of 5 points is assumed to represent the basic expected performance or past performance obtained from historical records.

The other scales, for the other factors, are similar in concept and each awards points on a 0 to 10 scale (for quality, the bands are based on reject rates; for

Table 5.1 Factor scale

Output band (in terms of average standard hours of work completed per week)	Points awarded
450 or over	10
440–449	9
430–439	8
415–429	7
400–414	6
380–399	5
360–379	4
340–359	3
315–339	2
290–314	1
less than 290	0

absenteeism, on lateness and absence records; and for safety, on hours lost due to sickness (at work) and accidents). Because of the legal requirements on safety, this scale is very narrow and a high score is quite possible, and obviously encouraged.

The productivity index for the group is then calculated at the end of each four-week period as shown in Table 5.2.

Table 5.2 Four-week productivity index

Factor	Points awarded	Weighting	Weighted score
Output	6	50	300
Quality	7	25	175
Absenteeism	5	15	75
Safety	10	10	100

Total points score for current period = 650

Points score from last 4-week period = 630

Productivity index = $\dfrac{650}{630} \times 100 = 103$

The advantage of this relatively 'unscientific' approach is that it is suitable for many areas of activity where objective measures are not applicable. It is normally possible to identify factors that should be assessed (including top-line factors), to create a measurement scale – even if this has to be based on subjective judgements – and to decide on relative weightings. If this can be done, then a productivity index can be derived as the basis of measuring subsequent success in productivity improvement.

Similarly the Tri-Hire example shows the use of performance (rather than productivity) measures relating to customer satisfaction. The measures of customer satisfaction contribute to the revenue productivity index and thus satisfy our requirement that measures at a lower level should contribute to a higher-level measure, and to organisational objectives.

The importance of including top-line factors in a measurement programme does not negate the use of more 'traditional' measures. We have claimed, as an advantage for the concept of top-line productivity, that it addresses both sides of the productivity ratio – thus resources, and costs, consumed are important. So measures, and measurement techniques, associated with such matters as labour performance are still valid as part of the total measurement regime. These measures should be group measures, used both for performance measurement and for planning and control purposes. Because we are treating productivity as an issue to be continually addressed everywhere, the measurement process itself should be 'efficient'. Consideration should therefore be given to investigating and evaluating some of the newer measurement techniques that can be applied easily and cost effectively to give data which is accurate and reliable enough for its intended use. A number of these techniques are also carried out on a participative basis between specialist staff and the employees whose work is being measured; such techniques should fit more comfortably within a top-line productivity culture than some of the older techniques, which are often 'mechanical' in nature and applied 'from above'. An example of one of these more modern techniques is the use of APT data, which is a simplified office work measurement technique.[1] See Chapter 8 on productivity techniques for more information on work measurement.

All that is required to establish an effective productivity measurement regime is an understanding of the concepts, a complete understanding of what the organisation wishes to achieve, and a little imagination.

Keynotes

The overall consideration is that we can identify and measure progress towards the objectives laid down in our corporate strategy and plan.

A productivity and performance review attempts to define the range and nature of any current measures used to assess and evaluate productivity or performance within parts of or the whole of the organisation.

The next stage is to review these measures and identify which of them are being used, or are capable of being used, to change performance to offer more effective progress towards organisational goals.

The heart of a top-line productivity improvement programme lies in the approach taken and not in the quantitative assessment of productivity. Measures, as we have seen, are useful, however, in measuring progress and in maintaining motivation.

With a little ingenuity it should be possible to create suitable measures for the criteria identified as having the major impact on the purchasing decisions of our customers.

Once the organisation has established a measurement regime, it should consider the setting of targets for future performance.

It is normally possible to identify factors that should be assessed (including top-line factors), to create a measurement scale (even if this has to be based on subjective judgements) and to decide on relative weightings. If this can be done, then a performance or productivity index can be derived as the basis of measuring subsequent success in productivity improvement.

Discussion topics
In many organisations performance is both inaccurately measured and over-measured.

Performance and productivity measures nearly always result in behavioural change – but not necessarily in desired directions.

One of the problems with any measurement regime is that people strive to beat the last period figure or the new period target – just!

Reference
1 Walker, C. and Russell, G. (1989) 'An APT approach to staffing studies', *Management Services*, Vol. 33 No. 12, pp. 6–8, December.

PART THREE

Factors affecting productivity

Introduction

We now know what top-line productivity is, and how to measure it. It is time to address the issue of how to improve it. Improving productivity means improving all aspects of the organisation: the technologies in use, the structures, the systems and procedures, and the people. It is important to make proper use of technology – not to use high technology for its own sake, but to remain aware of available and emerging technologies and make rational decisions as to what to adopt and when to adopt it.

Organisational structures are especially important since they provide the basic potential for high productivity; inadequate or inappropriate structures mitigate against productivity improvement. It is necessary to examine the structures at both macro and micro level and create an organisation with a high potential for productivity improvement, before introducing any specific improvement programme.

6 The influence of technology

Chapter 3 referred to the increasing rate of change, and of resultant uncertainty, that shapes the environment in which organisations must operate. One of the significant items in the list of external change factors was technology. This book is not primarily concerned with technology as a means of raising productivity, but it must recognise that there is no one answer to productivity improvement and that technological change is one avenue for investigation – an avenue that must be followed as part of a total and ongoing commitment to productivity improvement.

All organisations operate through a mix of technology, systems and people. The technology may be simple and cheap ((hand tools, typewriters, etc.) or complex and expensive (robots, computers, etc.) but it exists in all organisations. There is a tendency, in some areas, to feel that high technology is essential and that organisations that do not employ it are necessarily less productive. This is particularly true in the computing field, where organisations that manage to exist with computers that are more than two or three years old, or worse still without any computers at all, are regarded as backward, old-fashioned and possibly dying. The rate of change in computers is tremendous: each supplier will have a new model on the market at six-monthly intervals. Yet the true rate of technological change is actually quite slow. Today's computers are little different from yesterday's – the memory is greater, the disc drives are of larger capacity, but the essential technology remains remarkably similar. The approach of computer manufacturers and suppliers to selling computers is like that of car manufacturers: new models must look different from previous ones, and some of the supporting technology is different (electronic ignition, central locking systems and so on), but the car of today does the same essential job as the car of yesterday, and in much the same way. The 'technology' changes are largely confined to supporting functions, and many of the changes are not technological at all but changes in the number of features. Such changes are not even functional changes when one considers the primary function of the motorcar.

This is not to decry or deny the advance of technology; major steps do take place constantly. Neither is it to decry the process of adding features to a product that makes it more attractive to potential customers – that is an essential part of a top-line productivity improvement programme since it directly increases the productivity numerator – but technology must be appropriate and it must be cost-effective; high-powered, full-featured computers are not needed to carry out routine word processing. 'Old' technology can be served to customers in an appropriate way – as proved by Amstrad when it launched its range of PCW word processors. These were based on a processor and operating system that were rapidly becoming obsolete, yet the full package offered appropriate functionality at an attractive price.

Technological adoption is determined by the ability of an organisation to make that adoption. Technology relates to the systems and people that surround it. Some technologies are not appropriate for some organisations because the technologies are not mature and robust enough to be adopted without a degree of support from within the organisation, or at a cost from an external support agency. As an example, local area networks (LAN) to link together the growing numbers of personal computers in many organisations have been around for many years. It is only now, however, that the technology has reached a level of maturity whereby naive users can buy a 'shrink-wrapped', plug-in-and-go package which will work from day one without significant support. Even simple technological changes will have implications for the supporting systems and procedures, for the way in which the people who have to use the technology have to work and the ways in which people relate to one another. Introducing technology is rarely as simple as changing one old technology for a newer one and continuing as before. Technology can benefit users; it can also be a burden, and it is thus essential to 'think through' the organisational and personal implications of implementing new technology.

Implications of change

Organisations must be aware of technological change, which has three main implications. Change may pose a threat to existing products that are rendered obsolete or redundant through new technology that offers the same functionality in a different package; change may offer an opportunity for an organisation to revise its own product range to take advantage of a technological breakthrough; and, finally, change may offer an opportunity to undertake process review – the way in which the organisation performs some of its essential tasks.

The first two implications are essentially for the marketing department to consider; the product review and rationalisation process must be informed by a thorough knowledge of available and emerging technologies. One factor is particularly important in that it assists in determining the *productivity* of organisations. This factor is the 'clustering' of organisations that often occurs around a high-technology organisation. In the past, clustering has appeared around areas of natural resource – such as iron ore or coal – and has been seen most recently as clusters of organisations around oil industry service areas such as Aberdeen. Clustering can be an important factor in determining the success of smaller industries. For example, in Scotland there is a woollen industry built around a number of small to medium-sized companies. Each of those companies is unable to make the investment in some of the supporting services that can improve productivity. If such services cannot be provided by a company that is part of the local cluster, the productivity and competitiveness of all the organisations is threatened. Technological development may provide an opportunity for the establishment of such a supporting service to a cluster of such small organisations.

The third implication – that of opportunity for process review – is the one that may have a major impact on traditional forms of productivity improvement, cost cutting and output raising. The kind of productivity improvement programme that is described in this book is one of continual review and change; that review and change must include the technological environment. The programme places great emphasis on the contribution of employees to productivity improvement, but here is one area where specialist support is essential.

Technological changes are normally introduced in one of two ways. Firstly, in tackling particular problems or situations, whoever is responsible for the investigation is called upon to review the technology that is available to solve the problem or improve the situation. Thus, a production engineer who is examining the problem of old, unreliable machinery used in a vital stage of the manufacturing process will examine what has become available since that technology was implemented and compare the present and alternative technologies. Similarly a review of warehouse and distribution operations will require the study of advanced warehousing, palletisation, transportation and so on. Secondly, in most organisations, some form of technology monitoring or scanning is in place that causes new technologies to be considered, even where no formal investigation has been instigated. This scanning process in many organisations is no more than 'professional' staff reading their professional journals and trade magazines; in others it may be a formal process as part of the corporate planning, research and development or marketing functions. It is essential that some form of scanning goes on – and, since it is essential, there should be some formal process that requires it to be done. Again this formal process may simply mean the allocation of a staff development budget which ensures that key staff are able to attend appropriate courses and seminars; but the system should require, or at least encourage, them to prepare a report on relevant, or potentially relevant, technological advances that may have stronger implications for colleagues in other areas. Thus, a seminar update newsletter could be circulated or lodged in the library with short abstracts being circulated to allow faster scanning.

The assessment of technology obviously means that its financial viability should be measured. There are well-established procedures for doing this, but it is important that all factors are included in the evaluation, especially the ongoing, life-cycle costs associated with the technology. When examining the effects of technology on productivity, it is important that labour productivity is not singled out for consideration. Much modern technology reduces the labour input to a process, yet a full multifactor productivity measurement process may indicate that overall productivity does not necessarily rise. It is important that this overall productivity is assessed and evaluated.

Technology scanning

Technology is no longer simply concerned with equipment or hardware; software and methodologies are now so inextricably linked with hardware that they can be considered technology developments. Thus, for example, Just-In-Time and Flexible Manufacturing Systems may manifest themselves as either or both of hardware and software (or procedural) changes. For the purposes of technology scanning, all can be regarded as technology changes; they will be reported and discussed in the same sources as straight hardware developments. Similarly, CAD/CAM and Software CASE (Computer Aided Software Engineering) are essentially software developments that would not be possible without the supporting hardware developments that gave rise to them: they are, again, essentially technology developments.

Since technological change has implications for productivity review and improvement, there should be a system of technological scanning as part of the overall commitment to productivity improvement. In a previous paragraph, it was suggested that 'product-based' scanning is part of the marketing function – this is to ensure that top-line value is enhanced, as appropriate, by utilising technology in the product range itself. The review of process technology is aimed at attacking the bottom line – the resource inputs; the aim here is to establish whether technological developments will enable the product or service to be delivered more (cost-)effectively. Thus technology has implications for both the numerator and denominator of the productivity ratio. The actual scanning process for marketing-led technology review and for process-led review may be combined to some degree; but what matters is that the organisation:

- monitors the environment for signs and signals that may be the forerunners of relevant technological change. For maximum advantage, especially in marketing and product-related areas, technological change must be recognised early. Early recognition does not necessarily mean early adoption; it may be that the organisation decides to wait and continue monitoring until some future time before adopting the technology;

- monitors the environment for evidence of stable technology which may offer opportunity for advantageous process change (the horror stories that abound about computer network installations serve to illustrate that process technology should be stable);

- makes an assessment of potential consequences. The nature of the technology and the situation determines the nature of this assessment. It may initially be a conceptual evaluation offering simple product concepts that could be based on the technology or describing the nature or process change that may result. Once the concepts have been discussed and approved, a second stage of feasibility and cost assessment must be undertaken;

- presents the information derived from the scanning process in a timely and appropriate manner to those with the responsibility for decision making.

In terms of process change, this could, at a simple level, be the purchasing officer making regular surveys of particular relevant areas and presenting information on trends in, say, office equipment together with information from external agencies on criteria to be addressed when considering the purchase of such equipment. (This may be circumvented to some degree by making use of existing commercial services which produce technological and purchasing reports for particular technologies or industries.) This information can be fed on a regular basis to departmental managers for them to consider as part of their normal operational review process and perhaps be combined with the aforementioned seminar update to form a Technology Review Newsletter. At a more sophisticated level it may involve the creation of 'technology teams' to meet on a regular basis and to share information and ideas on new technologies.

Technology may be a major part of the responsibility of research and development departments (R&D) but often they are primarily concerned with a specific type of technology or technology for a particular area. There must therefore be a wider involvement, perhaps by having technology review meetings at which R&D staff meet with production and process engineers, management services staff and line managers to view the wider context of technology. Such a process serves a number of aims: besides offering a contribution to the technology monitoring process, it serves as a development opportunity for those involved and assists the breakdown of interdepartmental barriers.

If such technological scanning and reporting is carried out effectively, it provides a service to the overall productivity improvement programme. When specific situations are raised, either by the management of the organisation or by the employees, it may be necessary to initiate a project in which support staff investigate the situation or suggestion raised and report on feasibility, cost and so forth of making (identified) changes. Where such staff have access to already compiled technology reports or can use 'expert' staff as a discussion group, the investigation is likely to be more effective, cheaper and quicker.

Of course, in addition to carrying out technological scanning of the external environment, many organisations will have an in-house technology development service. This will most commonly be in the form of an R&D department but could be part of an engineering or other function. Only in large organisations will there be true, first-order technological breakthroughs: the advantage of such a breakthrough is that the organisation has exclusive access to the new technology and will be able to use it directly or license it to others. Most organisations take up such first-order developments that have been developed elsewhere; the aim is to build on such primary breakthroughs and use them to develop second-order innovations. Where an organisation is too small to have the resources to undertake primary research, it may be possible to forge some form of partnership with another organisation: such links are becoming common beetween medium-sized firms and academic institutions where the firm sponsors a research programme within the institution and then has access to the results for its own development programme.

The rest of this book is aimed at providing structures, systems and procedures that fit together to offer an organisation a high potential for productivity improvement. Technological scanning and the development and adoption of appropriate technologies both as part of product and process development must sit alongside this 'structural' solution as part of the total commitment to productivity improvement.

This approach to productivity improvement generally follows a top-down approach. Technology changes arise from managerial decision making. The productivity improvement programme thus consists of a number of strands – of which technology is one. The role of the management is to ensure that these strands knit together as part of one comprehensive and co-ordinated programme that accepts and encourages both top-down and bottom-up approaches.

Keynotes

Even simple technological changes will have implications for the supporting systems and procedures, for the way in which the people who have to use the technology have to work and the ways in which people relate to one another.

Technological change may pose a threat to existing products that are rendered obsolete or redundant through new technology that offers the same functionality in a different package; change may offer an opportunity for an organisation to revise its own product range to take advantage of a technological breakthrough; and, finally, change may offer an opportunity to undertake process review – the way in which the organisation performs some of its essential tasks.

It is essential that some form of technological scanning goes on; and, since it is essential, there should be some formal process that requires it to be done.

Technology has implications for both the numerator and denominator of the productivity ratio.

Technological scanning and the development and adoption of appropriate technologies both as part of product and process development must sit alongside this 'structural' solution as part of the total commitment to productivity improvement.

The role of management is to ensure that the various strands of the productivity improvement programme, including technology development, knit together as part of one comprehensive and co-ordinated programme that accepts and encourages both top-down and bottom-up approaches.

Discussion topics

Consider two or three home appliances (washing machine, hi-fi unit, etc.). List the technology changes that have taken place on a typical product over the last 5 or 10 years. Are the changes functional, service-based or ...? Is it possible to identify the source of the technology (a specific company – such as Sony for the personal stereo)?

Has that company taken full advantage of the technology breakthrough? What technology changes would you like to see in each of the appliances?

Why has the typical computer screen (80 columns by 25 lines) endured for so long, when most work carried out will eventually be printed on an A4 page? Is a technology change required?

7 The organisation structure

This chapter could equally have been entitled 'Creating an organisation for the twenty-first century'. The environment is changing, but, as we have already discussed, we are uncertain of how and how fast. One thing is sure: the ways in which organisations operate in 10 to 15 years' time will differ from the ways in which they operate now.

- Recent changes in Eastern Europe must lead to changing competitive pressures and changing co-operative opportunities.

- The countries of the Pacific Basin have demonstrated that whole industries can be grown from scratch in a short period of time.

- Capital knows no boundaries and organisations in the UK may be owned by conglomerates based in the USA, Japan, Europe or wherever.

In the face of these facts, it is quite remarkable that when the structures of a range of organisations in the UK in different industrial and commercial sectors are analysed, they are almost all the same. It is even more remarkable that such structures are the same as those organisations had 20, 30 or 40 years ago. We have tinkered with different organisation forms and work practices, such as flexitime and job sharing, but we have not been asking the basic questions.

- Should the changing environment not be reflected in the nature of our organisations and the way in which they are structured to carry out their tasks?

- Would changes be beneficial in terms of producing higher productivity?

- Why do we hold fast to the structures of the past?

- How can structure be made a catalyst of change and of improved productivity?

An effective top-line productivity measurement and improvement programme depends, in part, on the availability of sound data for use in the measurement, monitoring and control processes. All organisations create systems which are designed to produce, store and retrieve data, whether these are simple paper-based or complex computerised systems.

The past five years have seen the large-scale introduction of information technology (IT) into all forms of public and private sector organisations. (Information Technology Year seems a long way off; the technology is now in the mainstream of all industrial and commercial life.) This technology has been and is being used to support the capture, analysis and dissemination of a wide range of data and information. The result is the proliferation of information systems in support of organisational planning, operations and decision making. These information systems are the key to breaking out of the 'structure stranglehold': they make possible ways of working and co-operation that were not previously possible – ways that may cut across traditional functions and structures and may result in new communication paths and methods breaking through traditional functional boundaries and organisation structures. The phrase used was 'make possible'; unfortunately these possibilities have been largely ignored.

In order to understand something about the potential effects of information systems on the structure of organisations, it is necessary first to understand something about the common development of organisations as they grown.

Organisational growth

When an organisation, be it commercial, social, political or whatever, is first formed it is generally made up of a small number of people (perhaps only one) with a small range of supporting technologies. It usually has a clear, often single, purpose which, as it gets larger and possibly more 'pompous', will be referred to as its 'mission'. The newly formed organisation is likely to exist in one single location and to be controlled by one person, or a small number of people. The organisation can thus be described as geographically centralised (one site) and administratively centralised (small controlling group).

Decisions about current operations and future policy – normally relatively short-term decisions – are taken by the controlling group on the basis of the small amounts of relatively detailed information that arise from day-to-day operations, perhaps being 'topped up' with some simple research data. In the initial stages, because of the clear, single, central purpose and the 'newness' of the organisation in its chosen environment, decisions are likely to be relatively simple and short-term designed to establish a degree of stability; these decisions will involve the setting up of the structures and procedures necessary for day-to-day operation and planning for the immediate future.

If the organisation is successful in its chosen mission, there is likely to be pressure for growth and expansion. This will almost certainly result in additional staff being employed and in additional technologies (either more of the same, more variety or higher level) being used.

These additional employees may be 'duplicates' of existing staff, employed simply to increase throughput, or may be recruited to provide additional skills and expertise not currently present within the organisation. The process of specialisation has now begun. With specialisation of function will come the establishment of specialist information provision: finance 'systems', marketing 'systems', etc. Such systems will initially be operational systems designed to maintain the operating functions of the organisation, but eventually a demand will arise for 'management' information to support the longer-term planning aspirations of the controlling group. At this stage, the organisation may also see the employment of information specialists, probably in the form of computer specialists.

Further growth may result in a number of possible changes. Again additional staff will be recruited to support existing functions and additional specialist functions may be introduced. When numbers within one function become sufficient, a process of 'aggregation' occurs and sections or departments are formed under the functional title. With such 'departmentalisation' the initial controlling group may themselves be forced into accepting specific rather than overall responsibilities.

At the same time, in certain organisations, growth may take the form of geographic expansion into other sites, areas or even (in time) countries. This geographical decentralisation will possibly require the duplication of functions, positions and information systems that exist at the central site.

Sometime during this growth period it will probably be deemed necessary to draw up a formal statement of the organisation structure. This is most likely to happen at the end of a period of relative stability before the next growth spurt. The enshrining of the structure in text or chart form suggests that a process of 'ossification' has begun; the structure exists and will be added to, extended and marginally amended, but is unlikely to face radical change. See Case example 7.1.

Notice that at no time in this process did anyone ever sit down and attempt to decide on an appropriate structure for the organisation: in almost every case, it just grows. However, when an organisation is 'established' (and that may be a difficult term to define) the senior members of an organisation should periodically examine their structure and try to understand the reasons for its particular form and nature and to evaluate its success in helping to meet organisational aims.

Purpose of the organisation structure

An organisation structure, as we have seen, is rarely designed but it does get created from a series of decisions made, probably on an ad hoc basis, at each of the major growth points. The structure describes the relationships between functions, activities and between people. The purpose of a particular structure is to provide a means of co-ordinating the activities of different groups of people, with different knowledge, skills and specialisms, so that all are working towards a common goal. Within this the purpose of the structure is to provide control mechanisms, communication channels and separate focal points for suborganisation planning and the allocation of resources.

Case example 7.1

The degree to which different functional areas are separated from one another by the structure is illustrated by a recent training event with which this author was involved. This was a management game (or business simulation) run on a competitive basis with teams of six people from a number of organisations representing companies in a competitive manufacturing situation. The game was played over a number of rounds with those teams having the highest share price, calculated within the game software on the basis of a number of decisions taken by each team, going forward to the next round. One company had chosen to use the event as a training and team-building exercise for newly recruited staff (most had been with the company for about six months). The six people were chosen from six different departments of the organisation and only two of the six had met each other previously.

Over the period of the game they naturally got to know each other fairly well and were 'forced' to co-operate and to share information and ideas in support of their strategy formulation and decision making.

After the game had finished, the team members commented on the degree to which it was important to have full communication and co-operation between the different functional areas, and further commented that this was something that they did not perceive as happening at their place of work.

Determinants of organisation structure

The major determinants of structure are likely to be:

- the physical location of activities;

- the range/variety of activities;

- the traditions/culture operating within the particular industrial/commercial or other sector and within the organisation itself;

- the policy and preferred 'style' of the senior members of the organisation (based on those of the controlling group);

- human limitations, resulting in an assessment of such matters as the effective span of control;

- the technologies in use;

- the location of information sources;

- the legal, political and social framework of 'the environment';

- competitive pressures.

These factors inter-relate in a complex manner with dominance of particular factors varying from one organisation to another or from one time to another in the same organisation.

Since structures tend to grow rather than to be designed, notice that the organisational mission and strategy does not appear in this list of determinants. If we did attempt to design, or redesign, a structure and we assume that the fundamental purpose is to translate the mission or objective into an operating organisation, then the structure has to facilitate the four 'C's of:

- Co-ordination

- Cohesion

- Communication

- Control

and would have to take account of the determinants listed above.

In both these models, one of the most important factors is that of the information flows within the organisation – used as part of all the four 'C's. However, a brief mention of the importance of a fifth 'C' – culture – is relevant to the debate.

Organisation culture

'Organisation culture' is also a difficult term to define, but is a form of ideology, a pervasive set of shared beliefs, values and norms. The culture affects the way in which the organisation reacts to growth and it is both determined by and determining of the people employed within the organisation. It also affects the way in which the organisation treats the concept of productivity and specific programmes of productivity improvement.

The outward expression of the culture is the organisation structure. Different functions and activities within an organisation may be more suitable for and more effective under different types of culture, either because of the nature of the activities themselves or the nature of the employees carrying out that particular function at a particular time. However, the predominant culture of an organisation, determined by the controlling group, tends to result in a structure that pervades the whole organisation. This structure then itself fosters a standardisation of culture across the organisation. As a result, some parts of the organisation find themselves subjected to an alien and unsupportive culture.

If an employee within an organisation is faced with a decision for which there is no obvious precedent, the decision will be made according to the prevailing culture. If that prevailing culture is one of intolerance of failure, the decision will be cautious and made fearfully.

An awareness of the concept of organisation culture assists in the process of re-evaluating and redefining organisation structures and is essential to the implementation of radical productivity improvement programmes which demand the commitment of all members of the organisation. Organisational change carried out for a major productivity drive should be accompanied by an attempt to change the culture to one which is supportive of innovation and change. In fact, it can be argued that such activities as productivity improvement programmes, quality programmes, customer service programmes and their like are essentially vehicles for accomplishing culture change.

All organisations use information as a thread to bind the different parts together. Information systems develop as part of the operational and administrative activity of the organisation, partly through necessity, partly by 'accident' and partly by design. Information systems provide the data necessary for operational control, for managerial control and for planning purposes. Such systems are planned around the sources of data and the location of activities that need to make use of the output from the systems; the systems have to provide data at appropriate points in the organisation to support particular activities or decisions.

As the organisation grows, decision-making procedures often have to be devolved to wherever the supporting information is readily available. Information systems are often 'local', providing sufficient information of appropriate detail to meet 'local' need. This is particularly true of multisite operations, where certain decisions have to be made on the basis of local knowledge and experience of the local environment.

A degree of 'compartmentalisation' thus occurs with particular geographic or functional areas operating their own systems for their own purposes. See Case example 7.2.

Case example 7.2

Consider an organisation which wishes to reduce its material costs.

1   The designers, by the way in which they design the product, start the specification of materials.
2   Production engineers specify how much of each material is required, and may add to the specification.
3   Purchasing are responsible for the actual buying of the material, and may have a further contribution09 to the specification.
4   Manufacturing uses the materials (and creates scrap and waste).

So who is responsible for controlling material costs? Who has the information required to start the investigation?

Management Information (MI) systems may be superimposed at a different level to collect refined, summary data for higher-level planning and control, but such systems tend to be largely independent of the local systems. Information for productivity measurement and monitoring must be extracted from these 'local' systems. This may be relatively simple technically, but information is often jealously guarded by those who claim 'ownership' of it.

Impact of information-handling technologies

Continuing growth and development will probably see the introduction of information-handling technologies to serve these various information systems. Again, this can happen at a local level with relatively simple technology, such as photocopiers, microcomputers, word processors, etc., being used to automate existing manual/clerical information systems; or on a higher level with sophisticated technologies – mini/mainframe computers, networks, etc. – to provide centralised systems for certain 'important' functions like payroll and accounting. However, such technologies are generally introduced in response to relatively immediate, specific need and serve to support and strengthen existing structures and procedures.

Such traditional growth patterns tend to produce typical hierarchical structures, based on the pattern of functional specialisation outlined earlier. The 'compartmentalisation' referred to as evidenced by the establishment of 'local' information systems, produces a rigid structure with little lateral communication. Such rigid structures (often termed 'mechanistic') replace the more flexible 'organic' structures that existed when the organisation was small and new.

Organisational review

Although the organisation is now, hopefully, well established and stable, it must continue to review its activities to remain so; it must introduce new products or services, change the processes and procedures it uses to remain cost-effective and use appropriate new technologies to maintain competitive advantage. This review is rarely matched with a simultaneous review of the structure of the organisation. In reality the process of:

- specialisation;

- aggregation;

- departmentalisation; and

- compartmentalisation

normally ends at that stage, with little further review or change.

Unfortunately, typical hierarchical structures are often not very supportive of innovative developments, especially those involving the necessary co-operation of staff from different functional areas.

This is especially true in manufacturing organisations where the compartmentalised structure is very common and particular functional areas may see themselves as being in competition with each other for resources. Conversely, in many service industries, the distinction between 'manufacturing' and 'marketing' is often unclear: the customer may be involved in the manufacturing process, as when customers enter a fast-food establishment and place their orders directly, initiating the 'manufacturing' and 'distribution' processes. Yet, the same basic 'classical' organisation structure is normally used in both types of enterprise; only the names on the doors to each department will be different.

A number of alternative forms of organisation structure have been experimented with over time. One common alternative is that of the 'product-based' structure where the grouping of staff is according to the major product or product range (service may be substituted for product) and support functions are assigned to the product team. In large organisations this may result in specific product divisions on different sites; here the structure of each division may be large enough to include significant numbers of staff in each function – and so the hierarchical, function-based structure is simply repeated for each product division.

Attempts have been made to achieve 'the best of both worlds' by the use of mixed structures. One such structure, formalised within the literature and within some organisations, is the matrix structure.[1] In a matrix structure there will be the normal functional subdivisions, and running across these subdivisions is a product or project-based structure (Figure 7.1).

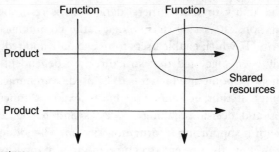

Figure 7.1 Matrix structure.

Such structures raise some problems – such issues as dual budgeting and duplicate responsibilities – and need strong commitment from the senior management team of the organisation who are above the matrix and must resolve any conflicts.

Another form of mixed structure is that of the parallel organisation. This concept of organisational dualism[2] is based on the notion that an organisation can have two forms of structure coexistent with one another. One is concerned with the mechanics of product or service delivery; the other with promoting and implementing change. Thus an organisation could have a formal hierarchical structure which is designed to make and sell the product or deliver the service, and a separate structure, with formal standing, to review activity and develop improved methods and practices. This may be a participative approach based on project teams, circles or some other grouping of interested staff.

It is not possible to cite one form or organisation structure as being inherently 'better' than another; what is required is an approach to dealing with structure that offers a degree of flexibility and that allows continuous or periodic change – within agreed parameters – to meet changing needs and changing environments.

New forms of structure

The means of providing this flexibility lies, in part, in the realms of information systems and technology. The technology used to support information services has itself changed considerably over the last 10 years. It is no coincidence that the term in general usage is now information technology (IT) as distinct from computing. IT is the result of the merging of computing and communications technologies. This changing technology allows a wider variety of information system provision.

The growth of the microcomputer (or personal computer) heralded a break from the traditional, centralised computing provision to dispersed, decentralised support of 'local' (generally fairly simple) information and decision support systems. This movement had the great benefit of taking the responsibility for information systems away from the 'experts' and putting it back in the hands of users. However, microcomputers, when used on a stand-alone basis, simply serve to reinforce the compartmentalisation and rigidity of organisation structures referred to earlier. Now that the microcomputer has 'come of age' we are seeing increasing demand from users for the ability to share others' data. This is resulting in the boom in networked installations. It is such technologies (the communications technology inherent in the term IT) which enable users to re-evaluate and redesign structures.

It has already been suggested that structures are dependent on the ability to place information at the point at which it is to be used: communications technology provides that ability. It thus becomes possible to examine functions, jobs, roles, inter-relationships and decision-making processes and to build an organisation structure along with a supporting information system. This design process can be carried out by examining the present structure and modifying it or by designing an 'ideal' structure from the above examination. In fact it is the second approach that is often more fruitful since it does not start from a predefined base which carries with it prior assumptions, expectations and allegiances. It is also this second approach that is rarely tried since the 'traditional' model of organisation is so deeply embedded in the psyche of most managers. This traditional model was, however, largely borrowed from that of the military organisation and can be considered inappropriate for many civil organisations. The re-examination of organisational purpose and the resulting 'construction' and implementation of a designed structure is 'organisational engineering'.[3]

With effective communications networks it becomes possible, though not necessarily desirable, to recentralise an organisation by centralising information provision. Equally it becomes possible to support a highly decentralised, dispersed and participative organisation. Information can be 'borrowed' by one function, department, project or activity from a pool 'owned' by another or from the central pool.

The typical hierarchical model normally includes a number of 'middle' managers. Senior managers of an organisation are concerned with long-term, strategic issues based on future uncertainties. Lower-level managers are normally concerned with face-to-face communications with employees and work groups. It is the middle managers who are often simply responsible for data and information flow; it is possible for new information systems to 'automate' a number of functions of the middle manager out of existence. Thus, even if we make no attempt to change the structure of our organisations in any 'revolutionary' sense, there is almost bound to be a gradual switch to flatter organisations, with fewer managerial levels.[4]

It also becomes possible to experiment with workplace and workstation redesign to offer alternative ways of working for individuals. Information can be made available at the lowest possible levels to support working arrangements that involve employees in decision making and planning functions that directly affect their own work. It becomes possible to improve 'the quality of working life' by offering the enriching factors that have been talked about (but rarely acted on) since the 1960s.

Where an organisation wishes to create a cross-functional, all-embracing productivity improvement programme, IT may offer assistance in breaking down the barriers between established departments or sections and building new alliances and allegiances. Naturally, the aim is to build a new structure that does not simply replace the old rigid structure with one of another type, but which provides an organic structure which can change with time as needs change.

Of course, in practice, this is not a simple matter to accomplish. The introduction of IT alone is certainly not sufficient. Many organisations build complex information systems on the basis of a divisional model which will be implemented in the same way in each division of the organisation. This has obvious benefits in terms of cost efficiency for the development stage and almost certainly makes it easier to consolidate information from the divisions for central accounting and planning. However, the information system may assume a particular form of organisation. Whether or not it actually demands the same form of organisation in each division, similar organisations are likely to be established by default.

Organisation structures should, however, take into account the nature of individuals and their ability to fit into a given structure. Thus there is a balance to be struck between the information systems and the structures.

This chapter has addressed both 'Information engineering' and 'Organisational engineering' since the two go hand in hand. However, traditionally trained information specialists are not always the appropriate personnel to create the necessary systems to support the kinds of cross-functional information flows and co-operation that we need to support a top-line productivity improvement programme. What is needed is a new breed of personnel who are capable of translating the productivity aims, policies and activities into measurement and monitoring procedures and then to translate these into information requirements. They must then have the appropriate skills to build information systems and organisation structures which together perform (or aid) the necessary activities in support of the declared policies and aims. Such a process may interfere with, amend or even destroy existing structures, relationships and 'power structures'. As such it must be handled with care and certainly must have total commitment (that word again!) from the senior members of the organisation. As with other such processes which affect the existing internal balance it is probable that they will be carried out by external consultants who are expected to be impartial.

The technology to support such a process largely exists. What is needed now is first the will to make it happen and secondly the skills to carry it through. These skills are only marginally concerned with technology – they are much more concerned with the ability to analyse business processes, understand productivity concepts and to identify information systems requirements. Ideally, what is required is a number of personnel with these analytical skills combined with a broad business knowledge and specialist knowledge of productivity techniques. Because we want commitment to the programme from the whole organisation, these 'specialists' must not be seen as the productivity improvement team but as the facilitators for the rest of the organisation. These personnel may be employed within specific functions or in a general support role but are unlikely to be career 'professionals' (e.g. career accountants, personnel officers or whatever). They should be capable of adopting a cross-functional stance, their allegiance being to the organisation rather than to any specific function or role. Together with the information systems they provide and/or use, they should contribute to the removal of departmental and functional barriers (the 'compartmentalisation' referred to earlier) and the shift towards a more organic organisation and a 'total' examination of productivity factors – including, naturally, top-line factors.

This lack of 'professional' or functional allegiance may contribute to a feeling of insecurity among such personnel. However, this should only occur in the initial stages before the new form of structure is accepted and before the new role is fully established and seen to be central to the future wellbeing of the organisation. Such feelings must be recognised and dealt with if the new approach is to be successful.

The kinds of changes we are discussing here will inevitably lead to a different form of organisation 'structure' than the typical, traditional hierarchy: it will work effectively only if the resulting 'structure' is capable of supporting organisational operations, special projects and future planning on a more effective and more flexible basis. Thus a future organisation chart could look something like that shown in Figure 7.2.

The information systems team and the productivity support team are essentially one and the same. There may be individuals with specific skills that could be designated as one rather than the other but, ideally, there should be one coherent team capable of providing a range of support services.

The resulting arrangement offers a framework from which teams involving these support personnel and operations personnel can be built to carry out specific activities or specific projects for a period of time, but can be reabsorbed into the 'pool' and redistributed to other activities or projects as the need arises.

The operations staff structure should be based on 'natural' groupings, around products, processes, material flow, information flow or some other linking mechan-

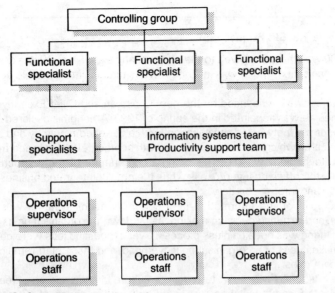

Figure 7.2 The 'fluid' structure.

ism. The groups should be as small as possible but may have resources added to the group for specific periods of time or particular projects. They will also supply resources to projects or initiatives driven through the operations structure by the support specialists. (The structure at this micro level will be discussed in more detail in Chapter 8.)

It is not possible to go further with a 'definitive' model since a structure must be built to meet the needs of a given organisation at a given time; and it must retain the flexibility required to keep it appropriate for an extended time period. The organisation must therefore be built, monitored, maintained and changed as necessary. See Case example 7.3.

Thus 'organisational engineering' is the planning and implementation of flexible, organisation-wide structures and information systems designed around the commitment to the top-line productivity improvement programme. However, to ensure that the potential is realised requires the full commitment of the senior management of the organisation, the development of a new breed of information systems analyst/provider, and a workforce which is capable of flexibility. There are a number of barriers to overcome before gaining acceptance of any new structure – especially one that is radically different from traditional structures. Such barriers will perhaps be created by the natural resistance to change of most human beings, by the established 'professional' structures surrounding current specialist functions and by the current scarcity of personnel with the requisite skills to fill the roles demanded by this form of structure. An organisation that wishes to experiment with such a fluid structure must do so carefully and with a supporting recruitment, training and staff development policy. It must also form plans and procedures to change attitudes of employed staff and to start to change the prevailing culture.

Case example 7.3 BP: Project 1990

Project 1990 was the name given to the restructuring exercise at BP designed to turn the giant organisation, which was in a no-growth situation, into a flexible, responsive business.

The project was announced by the new Chairman and Chief Executive, Robert Horton, when he was appointed in the spring of 1990. Among his declared aims was a desire to form a 'networked organisation' with a flattened hierarchy and a number of smallish teams which communicated one with another, effectively and frequently. Information technology was seen as being a cornerstone of the restructuring process, as was the office design process. Thus the project integrated business design, office design and information flow.

The purpose of the information (and communication) systems was to push information, and resulting decision making, as far down the organisation as possible. The restructuring was not a painless process: over a thousand jobs were cut at Head Office to make it less of an organisational overhead, and those staff remaining were assigned team roles.

The restructuring was seen to require a culture change and an extensive programme of staff communication was instituted with a series of 'Culture Team' roadshows used to spread the message to all operating units. The message was about the removal of bureaucracy and the assigning of responsibility. The organisation chart that resulted has no firm structure but consists of an identification of the various teams in broadly grouped areas.

The new breed of information/productivity specialists required are not the traditional methodology fundamentalists but hybrids dealing jointly with the information and the human resource. They therefore need to bear a combination of what are currently separate specialist perspectives such as systems analysis, productivity analysis, technology analysis and organisational development. The flexibility of structure must be matched with a flexibility of approach. Conventional 'hard', problem-centred, systems analysis should be tempered by a 'soft systems' approach to the design of structures, information systems and operating procedures.

Global organisation

What we have discussed so far essentially applies to the 'single-entity' company. Much of the discussion and many of the points made can be extended to the organisations operating in a global environment, but there are a number of additional, though similar, points which should be made to fill out the discussion. Where organisations operate on a global scale there are basically three ways in which they do so. These three basic structures have been more or less popular in different time periods. The first structure, popular in particular in the 1960s when globalisation first started to become a dominant strategy, is that of the multinational organisation. Multinationals tend to consist of a number of decentralised organisations operating almost independently but contributing to some central profit pool.

This degree of independence offered local responsiveness and yet failed to take full advantage of global co-operation. The second structure, popular in the 1970s, was based on an international strategy. Here, organisations were built around a central hub located in the headquarters country and supervising certain aspects of operation throughout the range of countries in which the organisation operates. These aspects would probably include basic technology so that similar products would be manufactured using similar plant and processes in each operating country. The basic products produced would still be supplied to customers in the country of manufacture and its natural satellites but there was a greater degree of centralised co-ordination and control, offering economies of scale. The third structure, which has become more popular over the last decade, has been to form a 'transnational' organisation with a global strategy. The transnational organisation is essentially a global network of companies each manufacturing components which together make up the entire product range. Manufacturing within any one country is specialised to take further advantages of scale, of specialism, of reduced training, etc. Particular manufacturing facilities may also be sited to take advantage of specific local natural resources. This form of structure is naturally most applicable where products can be delivered across national boundaries. The motor industry is the most obvious example of this form of structure, where a car assembled in a particular country may have its engine, its gearbox and other major components sourced in a number of other countries.

The future will probably see further development of this networked, global structure. It has already been suggested that we are moving from an era of standardisation to one of differentiation. This will require the transnational organisation to 'square the circle' by becoming, again, more responsive to local customer demands. That means, as with the single-entity organisation, that the transnational must be based on a structure that has information systems capable of identifying such local demands and manufacturing facilities that are flexible enough to meet them while retaining the benefits of national specialisation and large-scale economy. Again, technology is a major part of providing such organisations – both in terms of building the information systems to identify demand changes and to provide the data needed to control the flexible manufacturing systems required, and in terms of actually building manufacturing facilities which are inherently flexible.

Thus information systems are a major foundation of an alternative form of working – but a foundation which can provide and support more effective use of both the capital and the human resources of the organisation in pursuit of the goal of higher productivity.

Keynotes
Although in the past 50 years there have been significant and sometimes remarkable changes in the nature of organisations and in the environment in which they operate, the structures they employ have remained the same.

The organisation structure should promote:

Co-ordination;

Cohesion;

Communication; and

Control.

Typical, traditional hierarchical structures are not very supportive of innovative developments, especially those requiring the co-operation of staff from different functional areas.

What is required is an approach to dealing with structure that offers a degree of flexibility and that allows continuous or periodic change (within agreed parameters) to meet changing needs and changing environments.

We need a new breed of person, capable of translating the productivity aims, policies and activities into measurement and monitoring procedures, and then to translate these into information requirements.

Organisational engineering is the planning and implementation of flexible, organisation-wide structures and information systems designed around the commitment to the top-line productivity improvement programme.

The information systems are the foundation necessary to provide and support more effective use of the capital and human resources of the organisation in pursuit of the goal of higher productivity.

Discussion topics

In a changing environment, organisations need to keep policy and strategy under continuous review and to be able to make decisions and adjust plans quickly and effectively. To what extent are such abilities aided or hampered by a traditional hierarchical organisation and by the kind of fluid structure proposed in this chapter?

Does the establishment of a fluid organisation structure contravene any of the established 'principles' or organisation theory? If so, is this a reason for not adopting such a structure?

Does a major change in the structure of an organisation require a prior change in the organisation culture, or can the structural changes be used to create cultural change?

References

1 Lawrence, Kolodny and Davis (1982) 'The human side of the matrix', in M. L. Tushman and W. L. Moore (eds), *Readings in the management of innovation*. London: Pitman.

2 Goldstein, S. G. (1985) 'Organisational dualism and Quality Circles', *Academy of Management Review*, Vol. 10 No. 3, pp. 504–517.

3 Heap, J. P. (1989) *The management of innovation and design*. London: Cassell.

4 *The responsive organisation*. A report by Richard Brown and Colin Coulson-Thomas. London: British Institute of Management, 1989.

8 Micro-level organisation

Having built the foundation, in terms of a fluid or flexible organisation-wide structure, we now have to construct the rest of our organisation. This means moving from the macro level of the organisation down to the micro level of individual subunits and individual jobs. Taking the 'engineering' analogy a little further, once we have established a structure that we are confident will help us to use our resources – especially the human ones – in pursuit of organisational objectives and mission, we need to ensure that the individual parts of the structure are soundly built – in the same way that an architectural design is only successfully implemented when the foundations, walls, windows, doors, etc. are each built and installed to appropriate standards. Thus each subunit or grouping must be analysed to ensure that each micro structure is appropriate to the effective operation of the macro structure. The most important of the organisational building blocks are the employees and therefore the role of each one should be designed to be supportive of those activities and objectives to which they are intended to contribute. If we require and expect people to perform effectively, we must establish that their role offers them adequate reward (not necessarily financial). The use of the word 'role' and emphasis on designing roles for people rather than structures is deliberate in that it means that we do not build up something that resembles the inflexible, hierarchical structure from which we are trying to move away. People will be grouped together; not only is it impossible to avoid that, but we want to encourage teamwork. We want to avoid at the same time the building of barriers between these groupings; we need to encourage co-operative and collaborative ways of working between any formally established groups. Thus if we concentrate on the roles that people must fulfil, any 'structure' is simply a process of establishing appropriate and convenient groupings of individuals into working teams.

The 'standard' approach to micro-level job design has been that of rationalisation, based on the scientific management approach of F. W. Taylor. This basically has involved the breaking down of work into specific areas, and then the further breaking down of those areas into jobs involving skill specialisations. This has normally included a process of skill minimisation in order to reduce the dependence of the organisation on individual employees. An alternative description could be the basing of individuals on the lowest common skill denominator. The resultant job would be described in a high level of detail which would include the relationship

97

between the job and the equipment and tools (the technology) involved Such an approach often causes alienation of individuals from the organisation since they tend to feel powerless and without any degree of self-determination over their own job role (and with no real value or worth). This can be counterproductive in all senses of the word – resulting in output restriction, poor quality of production, lack of flexibility and absenteeism.

Further development of job design moved on to consider the job content; the human relations movement rediscovered the worker and his or her relationship to the work. The movement to increase job satisfaction arose and examined the nature of work and the satisfaction that arises from it. The most significant influences on performance, satisfaction and motivation were identified as being the content and structure of jobs rather than the conditions surrounding them.[1]

The continuing advancement of technology also renders such an approach ineffective and inappropriate in many situations. Where 'the job', in terms of furthering the product or service, used to consist largely of manual work with supporting equipment and tools, in many cases it now exists on a largely technological basis in which the technology carries out 'the job' and the workers are concerned with monitoring, supervising, maintaining and controlling. If the technology fails, the worker may have to diagnose a fault and either put it right or call on the services of a maintenance officer, technical specialist or higher-level supervisor. Thus the practical skills have in part been replaced with analytical and communication skills. The worker no longer has a job to perform but a role to fill. This role arises from an interaction between technical systems and social systems.

The 'human factors' approach, prevalent in the 1970s, identified a correlation between job role and job performance, where role includes such factors as job content, status, inter-relationships, nature and level of supervision, level of autonomy, and so on.

Changing job roles and designing new structures at this micro level is not simply a matter of retraining or splitting the overall numbers of people into convenient group sizes. There should be an effort to look at the problem at a number of levels:

- that of the individual worker;

- that of the work group;

- that of the organisation.

The organisational issues have largely been addressed at the micro level, but changes made and issues raised here may require some fine-tuning of the revised organisation-wide organisation.

At the level of the individual we should be attempting to create a role for each individual that offers a suitable reward in terms of the level of satisfaction perceived to accrue from undertaking that role. This will include some degree of status, which may simply mean making people aware of the importance of their own role to the

98

wider process. Each role should include some variety of work: monotony is very tiring and generally produces poor quality work and demotivated workers. Each role should also include some development aspects: individuals should see their own value increasing with time. Where the work itself does not automatically provide this, development can be included within the role (but outside of the task) through including the worker in other aspects of the organisation's activity. Quality circles, for example, provide a development path for workers involving training and value-enhancement.

These points largely agree with previous attempts to establish 'principles' for the design of individual jobs. One such list of principles[2] states that jobs should have:

- an optimum level of variety;

- an appropriate degree of repetitiveness;

- an appropriate degree of attention with accompanying mental absorption;

- an optimum level of responsibility for decisions and degree of discretion present;

- employee's control over their own job;

- the presence of goals and achievement feedback;

- perceived contribution to a socially useful product or service;

- opportunities for developing friendships;

- where dependent on others for task achievement some influence over the way work is carried out;

- perceived skill utilisation.

Naturally such a list begs questions about the use of words such as 'appropriate' and 'optimum' but it serves to illustrate the kinds of issues that must be considered when designing work for individuals if we want them to gain satisfaction and be motivated. A useful approach seems to be to attempt to identify a hierarchy of aims and objectives until one reaches the level where specific objectives can be set for specific individuals or groups. This objective will necessitate certain actions and will imply the use of certain tools, equipment, methods, etc.

Where possible we should also attempt to decouple workers and machines. Workers can be tied to machines geographically (they must continually be present in the vicinity of the machine in case something goes wrong), or by method (so that what they do is dictated precisely both in terms of what and when). This rigidity in effect makes the worker into a machine and demotivates.

A number of concepts have been established to attempt to define meaningful roles for employees and some of these were used as the basis of 'experiments' on particular organisations. Some of these experiments resulted in forms of organis-ation that have come to be established as 'formal' structures. One common approach has been that of designing work groups, and a popular one (in the literature) has been that of the autonomous work group; but there has been a misunderstanding that this was the only way to proceed. This is not the case, but the work group concept does require further investigation and consideration.

A work group approach fundamentally means the linking of individual roles into a group role and the establishment of mechanisms to co-ordinate the roles within a group and the groups within an organisation. One major advantage of group working is that it is much easier to establish objectives for a group than for an individual; it must therefore be easier to measure effectiveness of group activity than of individual activity. (Individual performance measures are normally related to output only; group measures can more readily include top-line factors.) Variations in the performance of individuals, when aggregated together, result in a smaller variation in group performance, since some of the variations will cancel each other out. Thus performance or productivity measures for a group are more easily com-pared over shorter time periods.

Autonomous working groups

Autonomous working groups are sets of employees that form a coherent group, involved in the production of a discrete, identifiable product or subassembly, or who provide a discrete service. This service may be an internal service delivered to a separate part of the organisation. The group, as the name suggests, retains a degree of autonomy over such things as the precise working process or methods, the allocation of specific jobs or roles to individuals within the group, work scheduling, etc., and may be assigned responsibility for its own quality assurance. The group obviously works within parameters and constraints laid down at the organisational level and is offered supporting services and, perhaps, some claim on additional resources. The important use of the term 'autonomy' means that the group must retain some responsibility for significant control over its own working. In order to be effective the group must be involved in the formulation of team/group goals includ-ing some quantitative and qualitative aspects. They must retain a degree of control over what they do or how they do it or their target performance. The items over which they retain control must be important to the group and they must feel a degree of success or failure over the achievement of targets or the application of knowledge or skills that are perceived to be of value to them. Additionally, the importance of their goals must correspond to the importance of organisational goals.

We have used the term 'ownership' when referring to the task of ensuring commitment to a productivity or quality programme; those responsible for making the programme work must feel ownership (rarely exclusive) of the situation. The same is true of work groups and their workplace. The group should feel a degree of ownership of their own workplace and the work they carry out within it. In order for this to be achieved, the group must be allowed to exercise control over certain aspects of the workplace, as well as over the work they carry out. This may be simple, allowing the group to have influence over the layout, the type of furniture installed and so on, and it may be more complex and more work-related by allowing the group to have control over such items as maintenance schedules and access.

The more recent developments of such types of group working, in the age of quality management and customer service, may be known as 'composite autonomous working groups'.[3] The advantages of the work group-based approach to an organisation is that it permits a focusing, especially by the workers themselves, on the end product of their labours rather than on the process or tasks performed. This parallels our desire to have performance measures related to output rather than process measures, and it is an attempt to make the working structure reflect the nature of the product or service rather than the more traditional approach to organisational design which is to design a structure based on functional specialism and 'organisational principles' and then to fit products/services and associated tasks into the structure. The work group approach has the following advantages:

- *Clarity of purpose.* Since the groups are based around their own specific part of the product or service for which they are responsible, all members of the group should be continually aware of their primary aim. Groups are generally also built around a specific geographic location, supervisory chain and/or communication system.

- *Standardised behavioural norms.* The clarity of purpose and the common background contribute to the establishment of a set of common attitudes, standards and norms. This generally makes communication easier and more effective and establishes a micro-level culture. It is important that jobs and roles are designed so that this micro-level culture is in harmony with the desired macro-level culture.

- *Recognition of skill breadth.* Normally a group consists of a mixture of workers with different knowledge and skills. These skills are complementary and should be perceived as such by the management team and, more importantly, by the group members themselves. If the group works in an effective and flexible way, there will be a transfer of skills from members of the group to each other, without the kinds of 'demarcation' dispute that may arise under more traditional organisational structures where the interdependence of individuals on each other is less obvious.

- *Greater flexibility.* The transfer of skills referred to above, which can be accelerated by the use of appropriate group supported and instigated training programmes, leads to an inherent flexibility that provides automatically coverage for periods of peak working, sickness, holidays, etc.

- *Focusing on results.* Since the management of the organisation has devolved certain responsibilities to the group, they naturally become much more concerned about the results of the group than about the means by which they are achieved. The dialogue between management and workers thus becomes results-oriented.

- *Team cohesion.* If the work group concept is effectively implemented and managed, the teams achieve a natural cohesion that is difficult to impose from the outside. This cohesion provides an internal interdependence and internal motivation. Cohesive groups intercommunicate more effectively and generally have higher job satisfaction levels and motivation. However, unless the group's aims and expectations coincide with those of the organisation, a cohesive group can form a platform for discontent.

- *Quality of working life.* Although improving the quality of working life may not be a prime aim of any restructuring or reorientation, it is a substantial side-effect – one which itself provides additional benefits to the organisation in terms of improvements in employee morale, loyalty and motivation.

In effect the use of this kind of work group approach fundamentally changes the nature of the organisation. This can be shown by a comparison of a traditional, hierarchical, functionally based structure with a work group-based structure. A traditional structure is shown in Figure 8.1 and a work group-based structure in Figure 8.2.

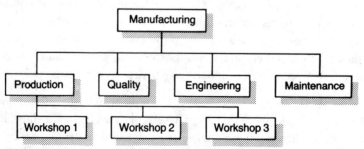

Figure 8.1 Traditional structure.

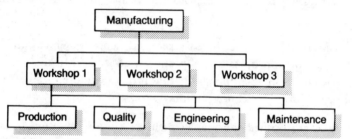

Figure 8.2 Work group structure.

Thus the focus is now on the production unit and the work groups within it, and each of those units is responsible for some degree of its own production, quality, engineering and maintenance. There will still have to be specialist sections to provide the expertise in these areas, but the fundamental change is to make these subservient – or supportive of – the production units directly. There is no weakening of the 'power and influence' of the specialist functions, but their role, and especially their communications processes, will have to change. As with supervisors under such an organisation, their role must be one of facilitating rather than directing. The Quality function is still responsible for defining quality criteria and assurance processes and procedures, but the day-to-day aspects of quality control pass over to the work groups who also make suggestions for quality improvement. This may be supported by the Quality function undertaking some periodic quality auditing to ensure that recommended procedures are adhered to. The central function is also responsible for evaluating customer perceptions of quality (perhaps a new role) and of translating these perceptions into policies, procedures and guidelines to be adopted and followed by the work groups.

Quality of working life
The quality of working life engendered is a composite of each of the other attributes listed above for work groups, and can be summarised as shown in Figure 8.3.

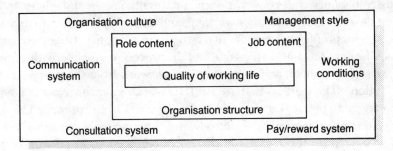

Figure 8.3 Quality of working life.

Naturally, the change to such a way of working is not without certain problems. New employees who come from a more traditionally structured organisation may find the structure and the underlying culture alien and may, indeed, be suspicious of the work group approach. Thus, induction procedures and induction training in particular, must be modified and strengthened. It may be that selection processes must be revised to ensure that potential employees are able to 'fit in' with the new ways of working. If the change to a work group-based structure is a phased implementation, some employees may perceive others as part of an elite group and frictions may occur. There will also be a 'two culture' organisation for some time which will itself create problems. Costs may rise, especially in the set-up phase, and

103

management may be faced with a 'test of nerve' to maintain commitment to the change in the settling-down phase where there will be problems of reorientation until the top-line productivity improvements start to manifest themselves. The nature of the management role must change along with the new structure. Middle managers in particular may feel threatened by the new methods since they probably have the largest change to undergo and thus 'the most to lose'. All of these problems can of course be handled as part of the implementation and maintenance of the work group approach – but only if they are first recognised as potential problems and treated accordingly.

One particular advantage of the autonomous working group in terms of a top-line productivity improvement programme is that it forms a natural basis for the formation of quality or productivity circles – a circle being a particular work group or an amalgam of a number of groups. The cohesion and sense of interdependence, the focusing on the product or service and the commitment to end results is already in place.

Additionally, group working increases the flexibility of the organisation – something which we have already stated is important in an age of increasing uncertainty and environmental change.

Even accepting that benefits can accrue from a change to work group structures, there are still problems to resolve. A fundamental one is that group working is not necessarily suitable for all types of production system. Machine-paced systems, such as flow assembly lines with conveyor pacing, naturally impose disciplines and constraints on the rates and methods of working, and the lack of freedom to individuals can cause serious problems. There are two basic approaches to solving these inherent problems. The first is to automate as much of the process as possible, with additional technology such as robots, and to remove human work from the process as far as this can be done. The workers that are left then work in a management or supervisory capacity and are not tied slavishly to the demands of the process. The second solution is to attempt decoupling by introducing buffer material areas to allow some freedom of operation; this essentially changes the process to being worker-paced. The associated costs, of extra stock and work-in-progress, may mean that this is an unacceptable solution.

Batch production systems, especially those organised on a functional basis where different classes of equipment are located together, are ideal for functional group working. However, although this may provide freedom over rates of working, it offers little scope for skill broadening and true autonomy. Where the functions can be brought together to work on a single product (a form of organisation traditionally associated with very large products which cannot be moved and termed 'construction' organisation, as for example in shipbuilding and heavy engineering), there is the greatest scope for true autonomous work group organisation.

Naturally, in all cases there is room for compromise. With a little imagination most of the systems can be modified to improve the role of individuals and groups, with the kind of attendant benefits that we have discussed. The well-known experiments at Volvo were just such an imaginative attempt at job design, in effect combining the machine-paced flow and construction organisations.

One advantage of product-oriented structures – where groups of workers contribute to a given end-product rather than being concerned with a part of the process on all products – is that it is easier to create a focus on quality. All those working on a given product can identify with the end quality of the results of their labours. If possible such an arrangement should be taken from delivery of materials to distribution of the final product, although for reasons of economy it may be necessary to pool products into a common warehouse.

If we put together the points made under the macro- and micro-level organisation discussions, we end up with a very broad outline structure based on the 'fluid structure' discussed earlier, and which is shown in Figure 8.4.

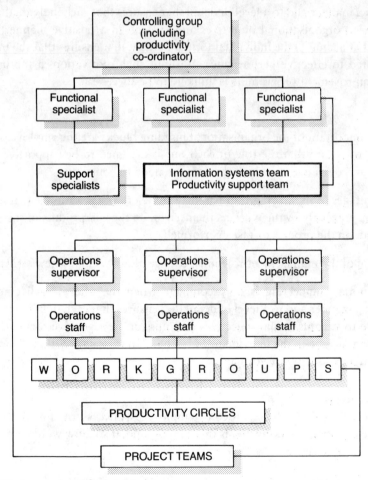

Figure 8.4 Work group-based fluid structure.

This is very much a 'conceptual' structure. Any actual structure must naturally take account of other supporting activities, and in some cases may not be too radically different from any existing structure. It is essential, however, to ensure that the structure remains flexible and both drives and responds to elements of the top-line productivity improvement programme. It must not build barriers, either similar to or different from those built under any previous structure, and above all it must be capable of working with the people who are going to populate it. That may mean that particular training or development for staff is required, in the same way that new staff entering an organisation go through some form of induction programme. The changes from any previous structure should be clearly explained and undertaken with consultation, with confidence, with clarity but absolutely. Although the structure may be less precise than alternative forms, it must be seen to be derived from a logical approach to meeting organisational aims and needs and as offering individuals a secure base for their future activity.

Organisational engineering is only complete when the role of each employee is defined in a manner and to a level of detail that ensures that each individual is able to contribute to organisational objectives and mission in a positive manner, and the rewards that accrue to the individual form a bargain that ensures that the individual is motivated to effective performance. Without such motivation, a top-line productivity improvement programme is unlikely to be successful.

Keynotes

The most important of the organisational building blocks are the employees and it is necessary to ensure that the role of each one is designed to be supportive of those activities and objectives to which they are intended to contribute.

The advantages of the work group-based approach to organisation is that it permits a focusing, especially by the workers themselves, on the end product of their labours rather than on the process or tasks performed.

The nature of the management role must change along with any new structure.

Organisational engineering is only complete when the role of each employee is defined in a manner and to a level of detail that ensures that each individual is able to contribute to organisational objectives and mission in a positive manner, and the rewards that accrue to the individual form a bargain that ensures that the individual is motivated to effective performance.

Discussion topics

Higher productivity can be regarded by employees as necessarily involving a reduction in the quality of working life. Is this a myth? and, if so, how would you disabuse employees of this view?

Do autonomous work groups take over the functions of managers?

Past attempts to organise workers at their place of work have been successful for a time but have been shown to have limitations. Why should the kind of approach shown above be any different?

References

1 Davis, L. E. and Taylor, J. T. (eds) (1979) *Design of jobs*, 2nd edition. Santa Monica, California: Goodyear Publishing.

2 Birchall, D. W. (1984) 'Work design', in T. Bentley (ed.) *The management services handbook*. Eastbourne: Holt, Rinehart & Winston.

3 Buchanan, D. A. and McCalman, J. (1989) *High performance work systems: The digital experience*. London: Routledge.

PART FOUR

Productivity Approaches

Introduction

Productivity techniques are not the core of a top-line productivity improvement programme, but of course they do have a part to play; as do other forms of programme which address one or more of the top-line factors. However, it is the basic commitment to productivity improvement and involvement of all sections of the organisation that are at the heart of such a programme. Productivity improvement is delivered through the workforce; it should also be delivered *by* the workforce. This part of the book introduces the various approaches that can be used in concert to attack productivity improvement across the whole organisation. These approaches are essentially means of harnessing people power. The final chapter in this section reminds us of the importance of this people power in productivity improvement, and raises the people issues that cannot be ignored if a productivity improvement programme is to have continuing success.

9 Productivity techniques

Top-line productivity improvement does not rely for its success on the application of specific productivity techniques: it depends much more on the commitment and creativity of all members of the organisation. However, such techniques cannot be ignored; they are useful as part of the armoury of approaches to improving productivity. They must not be regarded as the providers of improved productivity but as assisting agents in the process, a part of the overall approach. Ideally they should be provided by the productivity specialists for deployment by the operational staff and work groups. Such specialist staff thus become, correctly, providers of support services. One of the terms in general usage for such specialist staff is that of 'management services'. In the light of our desire to involve fully all members of the organisation, and not just managers, in our productivity improvement programme, perhaps another title is required. To represent their new role fully, perhaps 'productivity support officer' or 'productivity services officer' is more appropriate as a job title for such specialists.

There a number of approaches and techniques which have grown out of the productivity movement – work study, organisation and methods, operational research, etc. – and to deny or ignore their existence would be foolish. They must, though, be used as part of a structured and targeted campaign aimed at examining and improving all the relevant factors that contribute to top-line productivity. That means that they should not be employed in a mechanistic way but rather that the questioning and analytical approach they normally use should be harnessed together with the intuitive and creative approach that can be obtained through the motivation and enthusing of the workforce.

The approach and attitude to productivity improvement is much more important than the type or nature of any techniques employed. One of the great strengths of those properly and fully trained in the use of productivity techniques is the ability to question, in a systematic manner, all aspects of a particular situation, process or procedure. The fundamental questions of productivity improvement are:

- What?
  What are we trying to achieve?

- Why?

Why are we trying to achieve it?
What are the short- and long-term benefits?

- How?
  How might we set about achieving it?
  What alternative approaches exist?
  How do we evaluate alternatives?

These are supported by a second level of questions:

- Who?
  Who is responsible for a given objective?

- When?
  When will the objective (and subobjectives along the way) be achieved?

- Where?
  Where will activity in support of a given objective take place?

These questions are not asked in a simple linear way, but as a continuing spiral of questions as layers of a specific problem or situation are uncovered. Almost all the questions can be followed by Why? Why, for example, are we assigning responsibility to a given individual or group?; and almost all can be reused at the next level of discussion: What are the constraints? How can they be overcome?

For some tasks or projects, this questioning process may take only a few minutes. For others, some of the questions may require some form of investigation or study before answers can be given. The nature and level of the questioning process is dependent on the complexity and of the anticipated level of benefit accruing from revision of the situation under examination.

One particular variant of the general questioning technique that is worth specific mention is that of 'value analysis'. This traditionally is concerned with material analysis (component to finished goods) but the merit in discussing it within a top-line productivity improvement programme is that it makes specific reference to the term 'value'. It was one of the earliest techniques to make reference to the concept of a 'supplier' chain (which is another way of describing a customer chain) and, in its more sophisticated usage, encompasses the concepts of 'usage value' and 'esteem value', recognising that the total value attributed to an article or a component is a composite of its functionality and any additional perceived value. The technique attempts to address each material, component part and intermediate part of an article to question whether the cost of the part is commensurate with the value it adds to the finished product. Thus some parts may add functionality whereas others may contribute more to esteem value, perhaps through improving aesthetics or some other factor. Value analysis thus offers a framework for analysing a manufactured product and in particular its material content. One of the general aims of materials review is to establish the standardisation of materials and components over a product range in order to reduce purchasing costs, by taking advantage of economies of scale, and stock-holding costs. Value analysis can sometimes argue against standardisation if the perceived value offered by a non-standard material or component is greater than its additional cost. Such an alternative viewpoint offers an advantageous opinion to the debate and discussion.

Where work teams are themselves involved in the process of raising problems, making changes, contributing to discussions, etc. (as in quality or productivity circles), it is useful to have supporting agents to act as 'devil's advocate' by posing some of the above questions. The advantage of defining such support in the name of specific techniques is that it offers a structure and a credibility to a process that can otherwise be vague and ill-formed. The difficult part is to ask questions without appearing to be negative or critical. Thus, the approach should be to suggest that 'We need to ask Why or How or whatever' and then to make suggestions, based on experience and training of how such questions could be answered. It is also beneficial to offer training to the workforce in the basic approach and some of the basic techniques, so that communication with the specialist supporters is meaningful and effective.

Generally, training should start with approaches and concepts and move towards specific techniques where these can illustrate the general approach or where they are identified as having specific applicability within the environment of the particular organisation. The questioning approach so far discussed is so simple in concept that it can be used with immediate effect. The aim of this approach is basically to discover more about the nature of a given problem or situation. Doing this often leads naturally to the identification of improvements or beneficial changes, but it is important to concentrate on the situation or problem first without rushing into solution finding.

Thus we usually need to know something about the background to a problem since the immediate problem may be simply a symptom of some deeper, underlying problem. We also need to be aware of the level of dissatisfaction with a particular situation – dissatisfaction felt by different groups. Problems may be identified by an analytical study of past records, but such problems may not be associated with a high degree of dissatisfaction. However, where dissatisfaction does exist, it can be used as a motivating force in looking for solutions. Where dissatisfaction is felt by some group or agency within the organisation, but not by another (e.g. levels of overtime working may be increasing; this should result in dissatisfaction from the management of the organisation but may be considered as satisfactory by those undertaking the overtime and receiving payment for it) the situation must be handled with care. It is important that all those involved should have some (self-) interest in changing a particular situation.

We should be aware of the constraints that apply to a given problem investigation, whether technical, financial, organisational, legal or whatever. It is also important to identify which constraints are real and which are arbitrarily imposed.

Often managers produce terms of reference for an investigation with a set of constraints that have been imposed without real thought. The person or persons carrying out the investigation may, after the initial stages, feel that some of the constraints make the investigation too restrictive. Such constraints can be challenged on the basis of information discovered so far; others, which are genuine constraints, must be adhered to.

It can be seen that for many problems or situations, there may be a need to carry out investigative work on the problem and its environment before attempting to look for changes to be made. Such investigations may require the deployment of particular investigative and recording techniques, and it is here that support specialists can be of assistance in providing such information for the managing group of a given problem, whether this be a group of managers or a work group.

There are a number of 'methodologies' available to provide a framework for productivity analysis. In fact the questioning technique referred to above is probably the simplest and most effective methodology. Other methodologies are often proprietary, generally to particular consulting organisations, and may require the payment of some licence fee before being used.

The general approach of all methodologies is to find out what is currently happening, to examine potential solutions/changes, and to evaluate those potential solutions/changes according to defined criteria of success.

An important part of many methodologies is to attempt to identify what are the key factors in a given situation or problem. For example, in a commercial organisation, one necessary step is to identify the key factors influencing profitability. In effect, this is a form of sensitivity analysis. What effect on final profit figures is provided by:

- a 5 per cent wage rise?

- a 5 per cent material cost increase?

- a 10 per cent reduction in working capital?

In a capital-intensive organisation, the effects of labour cost changes may be minimal and it is naturally not in the interests of the organisation to devote excessive time and effort to schemes that reduce labour cost.

Pareto analysis is often a useful, and simple, approach to identifying priorities. One of its attractions is that its simplicity makes it an ideal 'technique' to be introduced quickly to members of the workforce who may be involved in some form of partnership that is addressing productivity issues – such as productivity circles or teams. They may possibly have heard of the 80/20 rule and, even if they have not, will accept the basic concept quite readily. Data which at first appear complex can often be more readily understood by presenting them graphically and then subjecting them to a Pareto analysis. Thus in an organisation which makes a large number of components to go into a large number of end products, an analysis which shows which products, and which components, contribute the lion's share of sales revenue can be quite illuminating.

One approach which helps to achieve a full picture of a given situation is to build up a 'family tree' structure starting from the existing situation or problem and the kind of improvement it is wished or hoped to make. This is expressed as a simple question. Taking a general problem, we may be part of a police force, local authority or other public service organisation discussing ways in which we can improve road safety in conditions of low visibility due to fog. Our basic question is therefore 'How can we reduce road accidents in fog?' This question is written in the centre of a sheet of paper and a simple tree structure created both above and below it, as in Figure 9.1. Above the basic question on the branches of the tree are then written questions

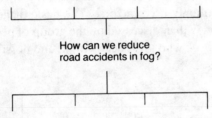

How can we reduce
road accidents in fog?

Figure 9.1 Simple tree structure.

that must be answered or tackled if the basic problem, as detailed within the central question, is ignored. Thus in this example, we may have problems of 'How can we detect the occurrence of accidents as quickly as possible? or 'How can we ensure that emergency vehicles can reach accidents safely and quickly?' If the basic problem is insoluble, at least in the short term, these 'above the line' questions offer the chance of minimising the effects.

On the branches below the basic question are written the questions that must be asked or tackled in order to make progress towards answering the basic question. Again, in this example, such questions may be:

How can we reduce the incidence of fog?
How can we improve street lighting?
How can we ensure vehicles do not travel too fast?

and so on.

These, in turn, may have subproblems (and therefore questions to be asked) and we add a branch under a particular question and move downwards, building a tree structure. As we move downwards, the questions being asked become more detailed and we inevitably move towards potential solutions, simply by continuing to ask questions.

The aim is to build the tree structure fairly quickly and then to examine it looking for questions that seem worthy of further development, looking for those that can be answered with few resources or in a short time, and so on. Eventually, the range of questions posed will lead to a shortlist of questions which if tackled will lead to the best chance of improving the situation or solving the problem. This technique has the advantage of being suitable for group work, allowing a group leader to build up the tree structure on a flip chart or overhead projector as the group pose the questions. It is also, like the basic questioning procedure, simple in concept and simple to apply.

A similar, if slightly more 'fashionable', technique is that of the cause and effect diagram. This is sometimes known as a fishbone diagram, because of its shape, or an Ishikawa diagram, after Dr Kaoru Ishikawa who is responsible for its development and promotion. This diagram takes a known, or desired, situation (the effect) and attempts to identify the factors influencing the situation (causes, and subcauses). Initially, at least, these factors are often common: people, equipment, methods and materials are four commonly used factors. (The basic diagram is shown in Figure 9.2.) Each of the factors is then discussed by the group of people responsible for the situation or, perhaps, those who must deal with it, and possible subfactors or causes are identified.

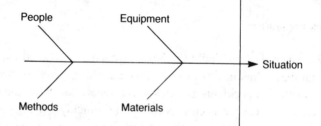

Figure 9.2 Cause and effect base diagram.

Consider the situation where a particular process is producing components of variable quality – identified, perhaps, by the use of quality control charts or simply by the comments of those who have to use the components in a subsequent process.

Under the 'People' factor, the group undertaking the examination may have subfactors, or possible causes of the final effect, of 'lack of training', 'working too fast', 'high labour turnover', and so on. The chart would thus look as in Figure 9.3.

This would be repeated for each of the other factors. Again, as with the family tree diagram, after two or three levels have been discussed and charted, discussion moves to consideration of probabilities of cause and probabilities of improvement if the particular subfactor is addressed. In this way, priorities for action or for further investigation are established.

Most of the really useful techniques are essentially simple – often so simple that they are almost expressions of 'common sense'. Within work study, there is a technique known as method study which is defined as:

Method study is the systematic recording and critical examination of existing and proposed ways of doing work, as a means of developing and applying easier and more effective methods and reducing costs.[1]

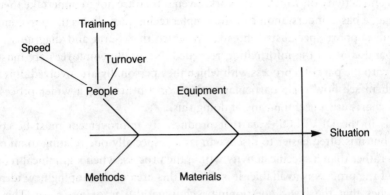

Figure 9.3 Cause and effect diagram.

Method study is based around a procedure known, not surprisingly, as the basis method study procedure, which in outline form is:

- SELECT the situation or problem to be examined.

- DEFINE that situation or problem.

- RECORD relevant data about it.

- EXAMINE the recorded data.

- DEVELOP fresh ideas and approaches.

- INSTALL a new working arrangement, process or procedure.

- MAINTAIN that new arrangement as standard practice.

This is a gross oversimplification of the many stages that are passed through in a full investigation, but it does serve to highlight the salient main steps and to demonstrate the essential simplicity of a procedure that can be used as the basis of complex investigations. Where it falls down is in representing the process as a mechanistic process in which a series of steps is followed in a rigid, linear fashion. It also tends to undervalue the 'DEVELOP' stage. Practitioners who have undergone method study training tend to spend a disproportionate time on the RECORD stage of the procedure, since there is a great range of recording techniques available (flow charts, travel charts, multiple activity charts, string diagrams, etc.) and these are essentially easy to carry out and are useful in 'padding out' reports. The data collection stage is not obviously an end in itself; it merely serves to underpin the development of new ideas and approaches.

However, the basic charting and diagrammatic techniques are useful to serve as communication devices. Most of them are also simple, and training can be given to employees to allow them to record (at least in outline or draft form) the kinds of process and activity on which they work. Even if they are not to undertake their own recording, a basic understanding of the simpler techniques allows them to communicate with support specialists who may produce the charts and diagrams and to discuss and confirm the information recorded. Naturally employees are most concerned with the part of a process with which they personally are involved. It is useful to let them see how their particular activity or job fits into a wider process and process charts are a useful means of doing this.

It is in the DEVELOP area that productivity improvement must be concentrated; but it is often easier to discuss an issue, especially one relating to an overall process rather than a specific activity within the process, when a graphical representation of the process is available. It is also in this area of developing new ideas and approaches that the basic questioning technique also is of most use. This basic approach may be supplemented with the use of specific creativity techniques such as brainstorming, attribute listing, morphological analysis and so on. But these are simply structured ways of developing the same kind of questioning approach. They are often useful in the kind of productivity improvement programmes that we are discussing since they are mainly group techniques which the specialist support individuals or circle leaders can use as the basis of formal sessions to expand group horizons and get them thinking outside of their normally narrow, existing confines. It is unfortunate that many of us are actually fairly poor at the art of thinking. There are a number of reasons for this, but one important reason seems to be that it is virtually excluded from most of the educational process and from most commercial and industrial organisations. Very few people are given time or freedom to think outside of the narrow channels which represent the highly structured thought processes of their mainstream activity. The use of creativity techniques is one way to overcome the resistance that people feel when asked to start thinking in wider and freer ways. They also serve to offer a mechanism for turning a group of individuals into a functioning group. As such they are useful vehicles for early meetings of quality or productivity circles.

Another reason for the general lack of creativity is that failure is rarely tolerated. This brings us back to the 'short-termism' that afflicts much of UK industry and commerce. The pressure to produce results in the short term limits the approaches that can be allowed to develop. Consider the case of a research surgeon who develops a new operating technique (as when heart transplants were first devised) and builds a team to carry out operations using the technique. If the first operation, or even the second or third, is a failure, it is unlikely that the surgeon himself will be branded a failure or that the operation and the technology surrounding it will be deemed unsuccessful and shelved. Yet, in a similar situation, that is what would happen to a businessman or an engineer. Success is judged by immediate results. The fear of failure is a very strong negative motivating force: it causes us not to trust ourselves, and not to trust those around us. Thus workers may not ask questions of their supervisor because they are worried about seeming incompetent. The negative influence of a single individual who is limited by a fear-driven culture is significant, but when merged with the fears of others, the collective influence can be dramatic.

Freedom to fail is a key ingredient of creativity. That is not to say that controls should not be imposed – but that failures should serve as building blocks and the source of lessons on the nature of failure and the ways in which future ideas and projects may be made to work. When developing new ideas, the aim should be to have a large enough portfolio so that the relatively few failures can be 'financed' by the successes. A basic respect for all ideas is essential.

This is particularly true if the workforce in general is to be asked to contribute to the productivity programme (and without such widespread involvement it is unlikely to be really effective). Any ideas and suggestions arising from such involvement must be treated with the greatest of respect. Most creativity techniques rely for their effectiveness on generating a large volume of ideas. At the early stages, there should be little evaluation of ideas, and when evaluation becomes appropriate it must be done in a positive manner whereby each idea or suggestion is examined for its merit rather than for its potential failings. The task of those responsible for the evaluation and further examination and development of ideas raised, which may be the specialist support individuals, is not easy. They must reject ideas in such a way that individuals who feel 'ownership' of the idea are not demotivated from further contribution. More likely, ideas will be modified in the development stage or left for a more appropriate time, rather than being rejected outright. If the whole process of group development is handled correctly, this problem is minimised.

Many of the techniques that are not aimed at the creation of ideas are directed to the provision of information – information to inform decisions about alternative ideas, ways of working, capital investment, etc. This is in part the province of productivity or management sciences. The term 'scientific management' is normally associated with the work of F. W. Taylor in the early part of this century. Taylor suggested that analytical and quantitative techniques could be used to provide a factual basis for the management process. Although present views on management are more complex and more varied, there is a place for such 'scientific' techniques in providing decision-support information. Some of the techniques are very simple to use. Others may be conceptually simple but difficult or time consuming to use in practice. These techniques may again need the employment of specialist staff, but it is worth repeating that such staff should be directed by those who are to use the information. These people, whether managers or workforce representatives or groups, must know enough about the nature of the technique and the information collected to be able to consider the information provided in an informed manner.

Evaluation of ideas/proposals is an area that is often overlooked. The most common method of evaluating a significant project is through a cost/benefit assessment where the various advantages accruing from the project are assessed (in financial terms where possible) and compared to the costs involved in making the necessary changes. For ideas which have not yet been formulated into a defined proposal, the situation is not quite so simple. Here, the techniques used may need to be as vague as the ideas themselves. The approach is, however, essentially the same. Some attempt must be made to determine:

- the benefits that will accrue;

- the probability of success;

- any 'side-effects' (negative or positive).

Simple ranking systems are often used; more sophisticated versions attach weightings to different factors. In a simple example of alternative new product development,[2] the product aims/objectives may be:

- to utilise existing spare production capacity;

- to increase company turnover (by x per cent);

- to improve the perceived public image of the organisation;

- to make use of an existing by-product;

- to complete an existing product range;

- to take advantage of a technical development;

- to maintain employment of the workforce.

These objectives are prioritised by assigning them numerical weightings. Product concepts are then evaluated in terms of how they meet each of the specified objectives – and again a subjective numerical assessment is assigned. An overall weighted value can then be determined by multiplying each objective priority by the satisfaction score. See Table 9.1.

Table 9.1 Product concepts

Product objective	Priority	Satisfaction score	Weighted value
Utilise spare capacity	3	3	9
To increase public awareness of the company name	1	2	2
To enter the retail market	2	4	8
Total weighted value for this concept = 19			

In some ways, the actual method – and its associated scoring system – is not important; the act of using any method and being forced to make numerical assessment forces whoever is carrying out the evaluation to think carefully about the proposal and its implications. Any points scoring is simply an expression of this thought process. In any case the subjective nature of the scoring must be borne in mind: there is a tendency to think that numbers are produced by objective or scientific processes and that numbers carry more weight than words.

Work measurement
One area that has often proved contentious in the past is that of work measurement. Work measurement is a useful technique for providing information about activity completion times, workloads, capacities and so on. Unfortunately, it has too often been linked to payment systems, and individual performance measures have been treated with antagonism by many workforces, with the measured times being incorporated into the wage negotiation system. Yet it is a useful technique (or more properly range of techniques, since there are a large number of techniques suitable for different types of work and work situations) with wide applicability within the planning and monitoring arenas. It must be employed with sensitivity. In a top-line productivity improvement programme, it can be used by particular groups to assist in their own determination and evaluation of alternative working patterns and procedures. If used in this way, at the request of work groups or teams, it can be established as a supporting rather than a damaging agent. Some of the newer techniques are particularly designed to provide data about group activity, workload and performance, and may be seen as less 'threatening' than those which are essentially aimed at individual measurement. Many of these techniques are based on predetermined times for particular classes of activity. The basic category of predetermined motion-time systems (PMTS) has been around for many years but most of the newer techniques are designed:

- **to be higher-order systems**. The basic and early systems give times for basic human movements (reach, grasp, move, etc.) according to the conditions under which the motion is made. Analysis of work into its constituent movements gives a very detailed record of the work and the times for each motion are assigned from a databank of values. Newer systems often use larger building blocks for particular categories of activity (the activity times having been built up from the base data) and thus offer quicker analysis times, but less detail.

- **to be computerised**. The analysis of work patterns is held on a database together with the time data for the system. When jobs change, through changes in working methods, updating of the times assigned to specific tasks is much faster.

These techniques avoid the rating of individual's observed performance that is associated with the traditional measurement of workers with a stopwatch and can be

121

more readily seen as supporters of a work group, in terms of providing information about the workload of the group and perhaps the way in which it is changing with time.

In the office environment use is made of self-logging or self-recording techniques. The simplest of these just ask the worker to record what he or she is doing at, say, 15-minute intervals throughout the day. Analysis of the results then gives useful information about the percentage of time devoted to each activity, and this information can be fed into the workload planning and scheduling system. More sophisticated versions make use of electronic recording techniques. For example, a recent innovation has been the use of bar code reading pens. Each activity is assigned a bar code and the pen is simply passed over the bar code (on a special sheet) for an activity when that activity is started. The start of one activity is taken as the end of the preceding one. The pen itself contains a timing device and thus activities and durations are recorded automatically. The memory contents of the pen are downloaded to a computer at the end of the working day and a complete, timed record of the worker's activity is available for printing out or for further analysis. Such self-recording techniques are not normally used in shopfloor situations but, when the time data are required by the workers themselves (perhaps because a productivity circle wishes to know the amount of time devoted to reworking scrapped materials), it is a possible solution which does not require the observation of the workers by people from outside of their own community.

More complex measurement, aimed at deriving standard times for specific jobs, almost certainly requires support specialists – most of the techniques require a degree of training and, especially, of experience if the results are to be reliable and used with confidence. These techniques can be employed by the support specialists to provide information that has been requested (explicitly or implicitly) by the productivity improvement circles and teams. Such techniques may require the support specialist to undertake a particular study, carry out some information-gathering exercise or analyse established data. Such projects can be carried out by the support specialist between team meetings.

Non-work measurement

Traditionally, as illustrated above, work measurement has been concerned with establishing consistent data on activity and job completion times, for comparative, control or payment purposes. Work measurement, with results expressed in time units, is important since time is a basic resource that incurs both actual cost (from what we do in the time and from 'overhead' charges that accrue in a time period) and opportunity cost, that is, what we could have done in the time. However, work does not use up all the time of an organisation; just as much, if not more, is used by non-work. When organisations undertake a study of throughput times for a given product, they are often horrified to discover that a given product may take, say, 20 hours to manufacture but 200 hours to progress from order to delivery. The rest of the time – the non-work time – is taken up by various delays, often in the form of (temporary) storage. It may thus be interesting, and advantageous, to undertake measurement of not just the work content of jobs, but the overall throughput times and to measure one as a percentage of the other. The size of the resulting figures may offer strong motivation for improvement.

We have not therefore ruled out the use of specialist productivity improvement techniques; we have simply relegated them to their proper place. They must be subservient to the process of establishing the correct level of commitment and the right attitude among all members of the organisation: and they must be used on behalf of those giving that commitment and demonstrating that attitude, not imposed upon them. Thus the specialist advisers may suggest the use of specific techniques and offer information on the nature of the technique and its applicability. If the group then decides to adopt a given technique to assist it in raising its productivity, the technique is much more likely to be successful if it is perceived as working for them rather than against them.

There are also techniques which can be used at organisational, rather than group, level to maintain the flow of ideas essential to a top-line productivity improvement programme. For example, in large organisations it is useful to be able to transfer ideas from one part of the organisation to another. Holding meetings of representatives from different parts of the organisation, especially where they may be geographically separated, is often too expensive in terms of both travel cost and travel time. One way of involving different parts of the organisation is to use the 'Delphi method'. In outline this is a process whereby a number of individuals are asked to think about a given situation or problem and to make comments and suggestions. This is often done by sending a questionnaire, or some other device requiring a structured response, from a central co-ordinating point. When the replies are received they are consolidated and sent out to the original contributors (anonymously), who thus see what others are thinking about the same problem or situation. This allows them to refine their own views and to recomment. In this way, a consensus often emerges representing the 'general' view of those involved. The Delphi method is normally associated with soliciting the views of 'experts' and thus, in an organisational context, would probably be most appropriate for the senior members of the organisation. It can thus be used for developing objectives and priorities. The method can also be used on an industry-wide or even national basis[3] as part of regional, national or industry sector planning.

Communication techniques

Communication skills and techniques are important for two reasons. Firstly, the above productivity concepts and techniques will be delivered to people who may find them unfamiliar and who have not been in any form of educational or training environment for some time. It is therefore important that issues and concepts are presented simply and thoroughly and that full explanations with numerous examples, of increasing complexity, are given. The trainers must be extremely good communicators and able to use the widest possible range of presentation techniques to get their messages across. Secondly, if productivity circles are asked to present issues, findings and results from their circle meetings, they themselves will need some training in communication and presentation skills and techniques. This training can be carried out as part of the general productivity training, since some of the presentation techniques will overlap with some of the data collection techniques – especially of charts, graphs and diagrams.

Keynotes
Top-line productivity improvement does not rely for its success on the application of specific productivity techniques.

The approach and attitude to productivity improvement is much more important than the type or nature of any techniques employed.

Generally, training should start with approaches and concepts and move towards specific techniques where these can illustrate the general approach or where they are identified as having specific applicability within the environment of the particular organisation.

The questioning approach is so simple in concept that it can be used with immediate effect.

Very few people are given time or freedom to think outside of the narrow channels which represent the highly structured thought processes of their mainstream activity.

Freedom to fail is a key ingredient of creativity.

Techniques may need the employment of specialist staff, but such staff should be directed by those who are to use the information.

Techniques must be subservient to the process of establishing the correct level of commitment and the right attitude among all members of the organisation.

Discussion topics
Discuss the problems of implementing a traditional productivity improvement programme within an office environment.

Discuss the suggestion that: 'Owing to the nature of the service provided, productivity increases within the local government sector must be achieved by cutting expenditure on services. Thus, top-line productivity improvement is not applicable to this area.'

How might a greater awareness of and commitment to environmental issues and the 'green movement' affect a productivity improvement programme?

Asking the workforce to be creative in addressing work-related issues will result either in a greater number of problems being raised, and thus increasing frustration, or in the workforce demanding higher pay for their new responsibilities.

References

1 Glossary of terms used in management services (1992). London: British Standards Institution.

2 Heap, J. P. (1989) *The management of innovation and design*. London: Cassell.

3 Ray, P. K. and Sahu, S. (1990) 'Productivity management in India: A Delphi study', *International Journal of Operations and Production Management*, Vol. 10 No. 5.

10 Quality improvement

Quality is perhaps the most important of the top-line factors; certainly it is the most 'fashionable' to deal with. Hardly a week goes by without some book or seminar extolling the virtues of total quality management. There is a danger that the hype will cause quality management to become another bandwagon which will roll for a limited time. Quality improvement is too important to treat superficially.

In any discussion of customer or client perceptions, the word 'quality' must loom large, but the issue of quality is itself a difficult one to deal with. It is difficult to define, yet most people understand what it is. Or do they? Manufacturers talk of quality in association with such measures as reject rates, scrap levels and so on. But such measures or other indices do not necessarily equate with the consumers' perceived judgement of the quality of the finished product in the marketplace. Sampling identifies only sample faults and errors. Even full inspection of every product only identifies those faults which the inspection process is designed to detect. Those items that fail our internal quality checks never reach the market (or, at least, not before identified faults have been rectified) and cannot therefore impinge on customers' views. These faults may not be what determines quality in the eyes of the customers. 'Quality' is more likely to be determined by customers as a combination of other top-line factors such as functionality, aesthetics, reliability and life-cycle. Thus to improve the customers' views of quality we have to do one of two things:

- add additional or enhanced top-line factors which will get a positive customer rating;

- ensure our products are free from defects and deficiencies which will get a negative customer rating.

With any one product it is difficult to determine, without extensive talking to customers and potential customers, whether it is the positive or negative factors that are the main determinant of quality. Ideally, just as with the productivity ratio, we should address both factors.

When considering top-line productivity, these customer or client perceptions are most important since they are the source of and rationale for any market expansion or premium price that may be charged compared to our competitors. See Case example 10.1.

Case example 10.1

If we are selling a motorcar that has a nominal base price (the average for the type of car on the market) of £12,000 we may, by adding particular features and by gaining a reputation for 'quality', be able to charge a premium of, say, £1,500. If we fail to add these features and also fail to maintain our quality image, we may be faced with having to offer our product to the market at a 'discount' price (of only £11,000) to maintain our market share. This gives us a £3,500 price gap based solely on the customers' views of our quality and value.

'Traditional' quality measures are both bottom-line factors in that they are generally a means of controlling and reducing wastage in the production process, and top-line factors in that they should lead to greater reliability of the finished product and a perception of quality from the consumer. It is important that we concentrate on the top-line nature of quality. This is unlikely to be improved by increasing the amount of quality control testing we do. Our intention should not be to identify more faults but to avoid creating those faults in the first place.

Although we are, rightly, concentrating our discussion on the customer, the concept of quality and quality improvement must move backwards through the manufacturing or delivery process to the supplied components and materials that form the basis of the product or service. See Figure 10.1.

Figure 10.1 Customer chain.

Quality is affected by all stages in the product (or service) delivery process and must be attacked at all such stages. This is one of the main factors in arguing for less quality inspection and more quality improvement. Inspection is often an end-of-process task. An organisation employs inspectors at the end of a production line or process to check that faulty goods do not enter the distribution network and end up with customers. If we do not have such inspection, the customer, in effect, becomes the inspector and identifies our errors. The chances are he will do that only once or twice; after that he no longer remains a customer. However, even if we do inspect, some errors will get through the inspection system. We can partially solve that problem by tightening up the system and employing more inspectors, to the point where every item is inspected and each one is inspected more than once. This is obviously very expensive. It also serves only to identify the errors. The process that is producing the errors remains unchanged. Hopefully, an analysis of the errors, if anyone bothers to conduct one, will identify the source or sources and attention can be paid to improving the system. It must, however, be more productive to start with process improvement as the goal and to establish procedures and mechanisms to bring about such improvements rather than hoping that they will arise from another (inspection) activity.

A common definition of quality is 'conformance to specification'. This rightly suggests that quality is more than 'goodness' and that it is measurable. It also suggests that quality does not depend on the position of the goods in a hierarchical market – it can apply to goods aimed at a low-end market where the specification may be less stringent. However, this definition still fails to take account of customer perceptions; the specification is essentially internal to the organisation, except perhaps in those industries such as engineering where the customer may draw up a specification for the supplier to meet. A better definition of quality may be 'conformance to customer requirements' – where the customer may be internal to the organisation.

One of the first things that should be done when attempting to initiate a quality revolution is to identify or determine the 'cost of quality' – or more properly, the cost of non-quality. This is more than simply the cost of waste materials. At best, it is such costs together with the indirect and administrative work used to support the production of non-quality goods. Often it includes considerable amounts of extra work to put things right (again including all the additional phone calls, retyping, unnecessary travel, etc. associated with the administrative and service functions). There is also the cost associated with identifying the faults produced – the inspection and quality control processes. At worst the cost includes the loss of existing or potential customers. See Figure 10.2.

Cost of producing errors
Cost of detecting errors
Cost of recovering errors
Warranty/guarantee costs
Cost of processing complaints
Cost of loss of goodwill

Figure 10.2 Cost of non-quality.

A number of studies, when aggregated, indicate that typical costs of non-quality in manufacturing and process-related organisations are in the range of 5–15 per cent of sales.[1]

When the full implication of such costs is acknowledged, it is much easier to motivate the management team of an organisation towards a quality improvement programme. Managers should also be made aware of the fact that improving quality by traditional quality control methods simply increases the costs of inspection, rework, etc., and does little to reduce the costs of waste materials.

The concept of 'cost of quality' is simple; but implementing this concept is often considerably more difficult. Identifying and quantifying the costs can be a significant exercise. A suggested method of arriving at cost of quality figures is as follows:

1   Select the business unit(s) or functions(s) to be measured. This may be by analysis of historical records, of existing quality measures or of strategic importance.

2   Identify the principal functional areas.

3   Select one of these areas for a pilot programme (preferably with high visibility and a high potential for 'success').

4   Establish a multifunctional group to undertake the project. This should consist of quality related staff, line management and management services support staff. It is also advisable to include representatives from the operating staff.

5   Provide the members of the group with cost of quality concept training.

6   Establish a project among the group members to identify cost of quality elements in the pilot area.

7   Establish data collection procedures (probably based mainly on historical records) to collect cost of quality data. Data collection procedures will need to be designed to fill in 'gaps' in historical records.

8   Charge the group with the production of a cost of quality report.

The aim is not an 'accounting system' that produces accurate data, but rather to produce a report which highlights areas of quality cost and provides data about the nature and level of such costs. If this cost can be related to the overall product (standard) cost and the selling price, so much the better, as the report can demonstrate what the customer pays for in terms of non-quality. These cost-of-quality measures can also be fed into the performance measurement process.

The 'new' approach to quality (armed with cost of quality information to both inform and motivate the organisation) is to concentrate on 'getting things right first time' – to switch attention to preventive rather than curative measures. Inspection can then be used, not to attempt to ensure quality, but as a means of confirming quality and of ensuring that quality improvement procedures are adhered to.

Quality circles

Recent years have seen the emergence of a number of initiatives in the realms of both quality and customer care. One example has been the interest in importing the concept of quality circles as practised within Japanese industry. A quality circle is a small number of employees, usually from the same work area, normally carrying out the same type of work or working on the same product or range. This team (or circle) meets on a regular basis within normal working hours to discuss issues which are perceived to affect the quantity or quality of work produced. In practice the range of areas and issues raised at the meetings is much wider than those that would be identified as directly affecting quality – though the quality of work is probably determined by many of these extraneous factors. Thus 'quality circle' is perhaps a misnomer and 'productivity circle' may be a more appropriate term. This range of wider issues discussed at quality circle meetings includes such things as the working environment, working methods and so on. The discussions, however, normally exclude issues connected with pay and conditions of service.

The success of the quality circle movement may be measured by the success of Japanese industry in world markets and the numbers of circles that operate within that industry. Many circles are registered with JUSE (Union of Japanese Scientists and Engineers) but many others are not. One estimate puts the number of active circles at 125,000 with a membership of 1,132,000 employees.[2]

Attendance at circle meetings is usually voluntary except for the circle leader, who would normally be a first-line supervisor from the work area. Where the supervisor is unwilling or unable to become the circle leader, another member should be given circle leader status, preferably with the agreement of the supervisor. This leader requires skills in leadership and in structured problem solving, skills which can be enhanced by the use of supporting 'professionals'.

Overall, the circles within an organisation are organised by some central staff member (the co-ordinator or facilitator) who also acts as liaison officer between the quality circles and the senior management. This co-ordinator must be selected with care since the success of the programme will largely depend on his commitment and enthusiasm. The person chosen must be in a fairly senior position within the organisation to demonstrate the organisation's commitment. He or she is responsible for the administration of the circles, for basic communication and for getting circle leaders together at regular intervals to discuss approaches, problems, etc. In those organisations that prefer mechanistic structures, this may be extended to the stage of having a Quality Circles Steering Committee which formalises the liaison role between the circles and the senior management team. The aim of any mechanism for such liaison is to formulate and review policy, to determine training needs, to give publicity to the programme, to receive reports and presentations from circles and to impose a degree of managerial control over the activities of the circles and the projects or issues that arise from their discussions.

Circles should not be asked to prepare formal minutes of their meetings but some reporting mechanism is needed to maintain an overall control over the activity. One way of achieving this is to hold debriefing meetings between the circle leader and the circles co-ordinator after each circle meeting and for the co-ordinator to compile a composite report on overall circle activity and progress for presentation to the steering committee. The co-operation of any trade unions in the quality circles programme is important and there may be a role for them to play in having representatives on this steering committee.

Depending on the nature of the organisation, circles that come up with suggestions to improve some aspect of the work in their own work area may either implement the change themselves – assuming it is within their budgetary discretion – or, more commonly, make recommendations to management. It is essential that any 'handing over' of data, problems, issues or concerns is done in such a way that both sides have confidence in the fact that the handover will lead to a real consideration of the matters involved. Some organisations impose a time limit (often very short, say up to 48 hours) for the reporting back to the circle or circle leader. This is part of the cultural change necessary to ensure that any participative activity such as quality circles will be effective.

Long-term view

The great Japanese quality movement is generally regarded as stemming from the work of W. Edwards Deming. In the late 1940s and 1950s he spent considerable time in Japan, working with the Union of Japanese Scientists and Engineers (JUSE) on statistical quality control techniques. Deming had worked in this area previously in the United States and had come to realise that by talking to scientists and engineers he was preaching to the wrong people. He needed to get at the decision makers and the controllers of resources. He arranged a meeting through the president of JUSE with an association of chief executives and, as a result of the interest created, within a short time he had preached his message to senior managers from most of Japan's largest industrial companies. JUSE themselves took up the Deming message and organised training courses for large numbers of people. In 1960 he became the first American to receive the Second Order of the Sacred Treasure, and the citation that accompanied the award attributed the rebirth of post-war Japanese industry to Deming's work. However, success was not instant and some of the Japanese found Deming's message and philosophy hard to accept at first. Two important factors allowed success to grow. One was that Japanese industry at that time had nothing to lose. The defeat in the war had left Japan with no confidence and an industry that had no pride in its output. Secondly, the Japanese do take a long-term view. They were not looking for immediate solutions. They were prepared to accept the ideas, to make them work through commitment and then to improve on them. The rest, as they say, is history.

Many of us can remember that in the immediate post-war years, goods produced by Japanese industry were considered to be of low quality but generally competitively priced (cheap and cheerful!). The long-term commitment to improving quality has led to the present-day perception that Japanese goods and Japanese manufacturing actually represent the epitome of quality manufacturing.

It seemed natural for the Western world to see this success of Japanese industry,

131

to note the commitment to quality and to attempt to transplant such ideas back into their own industry. The introduction of quality circles was part of this process.

Great claims have been made in the past for the improvements to be made through the use of quality circles, but in many organisations, in practice, such improvements are often not made. There are a number of possible reasons for this. One is the way in which Westerners treat new ideas. There has been a tendency within Western industry to look for panaceas – a single management or organis-ational technique that will transform organisations into 'super-organisations'. Thus, we have seen work study, operational research, management by objectives, job enrichment and many other initiatives being hailed as this panacea. Quality circles is simply another idea at the end of a very long list.

We, in the West, expect to 'plug in and go'

There is also the basic cultural difference. Although Japan adopted a philosophy laid down by a Westerner, they adopted it in their own way because of their own culture and traditions. This cultural difference extends to the culture found within commer-cial organisations, and the Japanese workforce, with its job-for-life tradition, was willing to follow the path of the participative approach to 'the greater good'. Western organisations have certainly been reluctant to follow the same path with the same degree of commitment and enthusiasm. Without that commitment and en-thusiasm, quality programmes of the quality circles form will not work.

Corning Glass is one of the American companies that did adopt a quality programme. Its approach was based on the philosophy of Philip Crosby, one of the 'quality gurus' who have emerged in the last 10 years.[3] One of Crosby's main tenets is that quality must be the province of everyone, whether they are involved in making goods, selling goods, carrying out research and development or administer-ing the organisation. Corning, however, found it necessary to supplement the quality circle approach with 'Action Teams' – facilitating teams of specialists who support those involved in the quality circle programme and discussions. Thus Corning Glass has taken a basic approach and tailored it to its own specific needs and circum-stances. It is important that support specialists like Philip Crosby, and indeed the co-ordinator himself, do not take over 'ownership' of any circle. For this reason, it may be wise to ensure that support staff remain with a particular circle only for the duration of a particular project where specific expertise is requested by the circle themselves.

When circles are first started, support specialists can offer a 'moving force', using their specialist knowledge and techniques to ensure that a programme of investigation and action is prepared and moved forward. As the circle members become aware of the nature of the items and areas under discussion, they will gain confidence and gradually start to increase their involvement and participation, at the same time reducing the need for the support staff to offer ideas and suggestions. The support staff can then revert to their proper role of providing a specialist service in support of the circle members. Where an organisation has no suitable support staff

132

or chooses not to use them in this facilitating role, other staff may need to be used to fulfil this important role of ensuring that the circles gain early momentum. This role may be assigned to circle leaders, co-ordinators or facilitators who will undergo training to ensure that they are able to handle the role, both in terms of raising suitable issues and ideas, and in ensuring that they do so without dominating the circle and inhibiting participation by other members.

In terms of assisting in the development of a top-line productivity improvement programme, quality circles (or productivity circles) are useful in a number of ways. The direct benefit of contributing to the improvement of quality and hence top-line productivity is one; but they are also useful means of developing staff and improving communications with staff. A number of organisations who have implemented a system of quality circles have commented on the degree to which they now have a vehicle for staff development and an opportunity to see those who are regarded as having potential for advancement exercising many of the skills that their new role will demand. In the longer term, it may be these 'fringe' benefits that turn out to be the most useful. As an example of this longer-term influence, the former American International Association of Quality Circles is now known as the Association for Quality and Participation, reflecting the degree to which circles promote participation by the workforce in the decision-making process of an organisation. Thus quality circles are:

- a form of participative management;
- a human-resource development technique; and
- a problem-solving forum.[4]

Those who have not witnessed quality circles at work often think that circle activity will be high during an initial phase when there are many existing problems to solve but that it must tail off as issues are addressed and the situation improved. This is similar to a commonly held view of productivity improvement in that it is largely a one-off exercise, and that given a reasonable timescale, an organisation can be transformed into a high-productivity organisation, a situation that becomes established and stable with no further need for improvement. If this does happen, and circle activity is concerned with solving a few immediately obvious problems, it is a sign that there has not been sufficient culture change – with a real commitment to quality or productivity improvement.

Total quality management (TQM)

TQM is one manifestation of the quality drive. It is difficult to define but is basically an attempt to dedicate the organisation and its employees to the continual review and improvement of all aspects of activity that can make a difference to the quality of its goods or services and the satisfaction of customer or client requirements. It is a team concept which requires a change in culture and attitude that puts quality and customer satisfaction at the top of every agenda and keeps it there over time, and retains long-term vision. Thus an organisation that implements a TQM programme may use quality circles as part of the effort to direct full attention on quality issues. In fact quality circles themselves stand a greater chance of being successful and making an effective contribution if they are part of a wider quality management programme.[5]

Often quality circles are the starting point for a culture change that enables the organisation to evolve into becoming a total quality organisation. TQM is thus similar in concept to a top-line productivity improvement programme; the latter simply is more far-reaching and addresses the denominator of the productivity ratio (the resources consumed) at the same time as the numerator (which includes quality and customer satisfaction). In practice, there is little difference between the two concepts since employees will raise issues and problems of productivity alongside the quality issues. The difference between a declared policy of TQM and top-line productivity is that 'extraneous' issues (of productivity) may be discouraged; and additionally that a TQM policy is often carried out as an act of faith without the measurement regime that is a fundamental part of the top-line productivity improvement programme.

BS 5750

BS 5750 is the quality accreditation standard supported by the British Standards Institution; in fact it is a set of standards which promulgate the ISO 9000 series of international standards for quality systems. Quality is defined as being fitness for purpose and safeness in use. The standard consists of a number of parts of which the most interesting and widely applicable is Part 1, relating to quality specifications for design, development, production, installation and servicing, when the requirements of goods are specified by the customer in terms of how they must perform and which are then provided by the supplier.

Organisations that seek accreditation under the standard must set out their quality policies, procedures and practices in a Quality Manual, showing how they comply with each clause of the standard, including:

- the management organisation, stating the duties of each member of the management team who has, within his role, a responsibility for quality determination: this naturally includes the Quality Manager. The arrangements for review of the system must be described together with formal audit procedures;

- (for manufacturing organisations) planning and fulfilment of an order, showing what is considered, who does what and how the necessary controls are developed and applied;

- how staff are recruited, trained and appraised;

- how suppliers and subcontractors are evaluated and appointed; how orders are placed and checked on receipt and how the performance of each supplier is reviewed and evaluated;

- the way in which the operational practices of the organisation are organised, showing what is done at each stage of the process of delivering the final product, and the way in which the quality of the delivered product is ensured and checked against the specification. Procedures for dealing with quality check failures must also be documented;

- the records that will be kept to show that the organisation has complied with the standard and within its own documented operational and quality procedures.

The accreditation is therefore not of the product but of the organisation's quality assurance processes; it demonstrates that the organisation has a set of procedures and controls that allow it to ensure the delivery of quality.

Thus BS 5750 is of most interest to suppliers of goods with a customer-driven specification. The standard sets out the way in which an organisation can establish, document and maintain an effective quality system which will demonstrate to customers that the organisation is committed to quality and able to supply goods to an agreed specification. In some areas of industry, conformance to the standard is becoming mandatory.[6]

It is not a substitute for a programme of (total) quality management. The danger is that BS 5750 can be approached as a mechanical process, rather than as a management philosophy. The Quality Manager may emerge from his ivory tower to issue procedures and make pronouncements, acting as a policeman and upsetting those who have to conform to the procedures. Over-reliance on BS 5750 accreditation to provide quality may lead to failure; it should be used to offer recognition to those who are driving the pursuit of high quality through some other quality programme.

One advantage of undergoing the process of applying for (and hopefully receiving) accreditation is that it forces the organisation to examine the ways in which it ensures quality in what it does. This provides an opportunity to raise issues of process improvement that may be more strongly addressed when there is a positive and relatively short-term aim (accreditation). Thus accreditation can be used to assist in the driving of quality awareness throughout the organisation. Even if carried out as an exercise in its own right, it should demand the same kinds of management and employee involvement, and management and employee training and development, as a fuller programme of Total Quality Management or Top-line Productivity Improvement.

Zero defects

Zero defects (ZD) is another of the buzzwords that surround the 'quality movement'. It is a concept that troubles some people – their argument being that perfection is impossible and that to aim for it is unrealistic. Yet ZD is not about perfection, at least not in terms of having a perfect product. It is about establishing the specification of a product which is realistic in terms of the market at which it is aimed and then attempting completely to meet – or exceed – that specification each time the product is produced. Thus a low-end product could be designed with a short lifespan; as long as the products that are produced meet that lifespan they are (at least with regard to that particular criterion) zero defect. It may be 'harder' to achieve the same rating for a higher-specification product. In such areas as aircraft components, however, very high specifications are issued – and met! Similarly with surgery-related products, defects are simply not acceptable. Higher-specification products require higher-specification processes, procedures and, perhaps, people. As long as these processes, procedures and people are appropriate to the specification of the product, zero defects should be achievable – not easily, but with effective preparation and planning, and good control systems. This should apply in all areas; but when we deal with non-critical areas, we get lax and start to accept tolerances around the specification. If we allow them, we get them.

Crosby, in conveying the concept of zero defects,[7] stresses the point that people do not inherently make mistakes or produce defective products. Mistakes are caused by two things: a lack of knowledge and a lack of attention. Both must be addressed and knowledge is the precursor of attention. Unless workers are aware of quality standards, the reasons underlying them, and the nature and causes of errors, they cannot be expected to be sufficiently motivated to maintain full attention. Armed with that knowledge, they will respond by paying attention to the quality of the work they perform.

All the initiatives and buzzwords essentially arrive at the same point: that quality is not really a function of the product, but of the organisation. Real quality comes from quality of process, of system, of procedure (including, if not especially, administrative systems and procedures), of people. If these are all right, the product quality takes care of itself!

Co-makership
Customer service programmes (see Chapter 11) rightly proclaim the importance of the customer–supplier chain. This chain extends both within and outside the organisation. One of the most effective ways of improving quality, and at the same time reducing the cost of non-quality, is to ensure that materials and components that are provided by suppliers are themselves of the highest quality and commensurate with the specification. Thus many Japanese organisations, rather than 'shopping around' for supplies according to the best (i.e. lowest) price available at a given time, aim to build up a long-term relationship with their suppliers and to co-operate in assuring the quality of supplied materials and components. This extended customer–supplier relationship is becoming known as 'co-makership' and is practised by UK companies such as Nissan.[8] The benefits of a co-makership strategy naturally include a developing improvement in quality of supplied materials, but also often include more efficient ordering procedures, better delivery schedules and improved information

systems. This might be achieved through investment, perhaps on a joint basis, in such things as electronic funds transfer, electronic data interchange, and so on.

Quality improvement is both a strategic and a tactical issue. It requires strategies and policies in place which over a long term address the fundamental issues of quality and associated costs. It also requires a commitment by everyone in the organisation to the continual improvement of quality. Quality improvement is thus a continuing process and is best attacked as part of an all-embracing development programme, such as provided by a top-line productivity improvement programme.

Keynotes

When considering top-line productivity, customer or client perceptions are most important since they are the source of and rationale for any market expansion or premium price that may be charged compared to our competitors.

Our intention should not be to identify more faults but to avoid creating those faults in the first place.

Typical costs of non-quality in manufacturing and process-related organisations are in the range of 5–15 per cent of sales.

Inspection should be used not to attempt to ensure quality, but as a means of confirming quality.

Quality circles are a form of participative management, a human-resource development technique and a problem-solving forum.

TQM is a team concept which requires a change in culture and attitude that puts quality and customer satisfaction at the top of every agenda and keeps it there over time, and retains long-term vision.

When we deal with non-critical areas, we get lax and start to accept tolerances around the specification. If we allow them, we get them.

Discussion topics

Customers are the only true measurers of quality; the tabloid newspapers are therefore the real quality press since they sell in large quantities.

In a well-managed organisation, there should be no need for formal quality improvement teams such as quality circles.

Co-makership is like putting all your eggs in the same basket, and therefore a dangerous policy.

References

1 Merino, D. N. (1990) 'Economics of quality: Choosing among prevention alternatives', *International Journal of Quality and Reliability Measurement*, Vol. 7 No. 3.

2 Wood, R., Hull, F. and Azumi, N. (1983) 'Evaluating quality circles: The American application', *California Management Review*, Vol. 26.

3 Crosby, P. B. (1979) *Quality is free: The art of making quality certain*. New York: McGraw-Hill.

4 Mohr, W. L. and Mohr, H. (1983) *Quality circles*. Wokingham: Addison-Wesley.

5 Russell, S. and Dale, B. (1989) 'Quality circles – A wider perspective'. Work Research Unit Occasional Paper 43.

6 BS 5750/ISO 9000:1987 *A positive contribution to better business*. Produced by BSI Quality Assurance and available through the DTI.

7 Crosby, P. B. (1984) *Quality without tears: The art of hassle-free management*. New York: McGraw-Hill.

8 *Co-makership: Developing the supplier relationship* (1990), Barrie G. Dale (ed.). Special issue of the *International Journal of Quality and Reliability Management*, Vol. 7 No. 1.

11 Customer service programmes

The parallel movement to that of quality management has been that of the Customer Care or the Customer Service Programme. This is essentially an alternative quality improvement programme aimed at the service sector rather than at manufacturing. The aim, similar to that of a quality improvement programme, is to consider the customer's perception of the service (which is often quite different from that of the supplier's) and to use that perception as a base-point from which to make improvements. It is wise to be continually reminded that the customer is the only legitimate judge of service quality.[1] Investigation is required to discover these customer perceptions of our offerings. In practice the concepts of total quality management and customer care are merging into a common philosophy, based on this concentration on customer requirements and perceptions, so that a manufacturing organisation may implement both Quality and Customer Service Programmes as part of a mission to identify and meet customer needs. Both are important elements of a top-line productivity improvement programme.

The best customer-related programmes go further than a simple concentration on 'the customer' in highlighting the fact that, especially in large organisations, intermediate departments or sections involved in the supply of a service are themselves customers of the primary providers. There is a front line in which staff have direct contact with the final purchasers of the service, and then a series of interfaces within the organisation where one member of staff, or a team, provides an internal service to another. There is thus a 'customer chain' which stretches back from the end (external) customer to the point at which our product or service is designed and specified. The frontline service can only be improved and maintained if all the other service points are improved and maintained in support. The frontline service is the nearest to the customer, but not necessarily the largest determinant of perceived good service. Within British Rail, for example, the ticket sellers, collectors, guards and porters provide the direct frontline contact with customers. Yet passengers' views on the quality of service are not determined to a major degree by their contact with these people. Passengers want, above all, the trains to run on time and fares to be at a level which to them offers 'value'. Smartening the uniforms of the frontline staff will have little impact on customers' perceptions of the quality of service. See Case example 11.1.

A number of organisations have heard of the concept of customer care and have

---

Case example 11.1

An example of a customer care programme is the British Airways programme en-titled 'In Pursuit of Excellence'. This followed the development of a new 'corporate identity' for British Airways, designed in 1984 – itself a commitment to realigning BA in the marketplace.

The basis of the programme was extensive market research to identify the discrepancies between BA's own staff's perception of their role in providing an airline service and the customers' expectations of what such a service should consist of. As a result, BA inaugurated a major training programme under the title of 'Putting the customer first – If we don't, someone else will'. The aim of the exercise was to get staff to accept 'ownership' of services and problems that arose within them, and to accept responsibility for improving the services and solving those problems.

As with quality circles, BA established a number of staff volunteer teams – 'Customer first teams' – to consider some of the services, additional services and ways of providing or improving such services. As part of the exercise, a 'Day in the life' event was organised to make staff aware of the operational procedures and problems of sections and departments other than their own.

In order to 'measure' the impact of the programme, BA undertook the start of an ongoing procedure to obtain feedback from customers, and the market research department currently interview some 150,000 passengers per year.

---

equated it with customer courtesy, but a programme of 'customer care' is something much more than 'smile training'. It is tempting the use the word 'obviously' in that sentence, but it appears that it is not obvious to many organisations. It is common to send frontline staff on training programmes that teach them to be pleasant and courteous to customers and yet ignore the real changes that must be made. A customer complaints section that deals with complainants in a friendly manner will do little to help the company image if the complaint is still not attended to in a manner perceived by the customer to be appropriate and effective. Dealing with complaints is important; but more important is their logging and monitoring to discover what aspects of the provided service (or product) cause complaints to be made, and the modification of the product or service design and delivery to avoid the repetition of such complaints. See Case example 11.2.

Case example 11.2

A customer bought a wardrobe from a retailer of 'flat-pack' furniture. When the customer got the pack home and took out the component parts, one was damaged. The customer returned to the store with the damaged part. The person who received the complaint was courteous and helpful, offering a replacement with no argument.

The customer returned home with a good, positive mental image of the organis-ation. Six weeks later the customer was still waiting for the replacement part to arrive and the positive image had been replaced by a much stronger negative one.

Customers do not want pleasant, bad service but they may prefer good service to be accompanied with a smile. Remember also that the number and type of complaints made by customers and the manner with which they are dealt is important; but dealing with these, analysing them and providing a better and more effective complaints handling procedure is not a policy of customer care. Many dissatisfied customers will not lodge a complaint – their complaint will be made to their friends and colleagues, other potential customers. One dissatisfied customer (who has made no complaint) may result in a large number of lost customers. The aim must be to remove the cause of complaints and such negative word-of-mouth communication.

The type of courtesy training often carried out may well have other disadvantages. For example, supermarket checkout operators sent on a customer care programme may be encouraged to have a 'friendly word' with customers while checking out their purchases. This could result in delays to other customers waiting in the queue and in some customers being offended by an 'over-familiar' approach. Each customer is an individual and must be treated as such. It may be that at busy times, the operators do not have the time to make an assessment of the customer and react accordingly. At slack periods, a chat with a pensioner buying a couple of items may be appropriate – but may have little effect on company performance.

Again, it is important to remember that the aim of a customer care or service programme is, through addressing customer care, to improve the performance of the organisation.

The problems of defining 'good' service can be further exemplified by the case of automatic teller machines (ATMs) introduced by banks and building societies over the past decade. ATMs were introduced to improve the speed of service for simple transactions and to provide a service outside of normal opening hours. In terms of customer reaction, they have been very effective. The additional service hours they provide has enabled customers to carry out banking transactions at times convenient to them. Indeed, many customers seem to prefer the use of such devices to dealing on a face-to-face basis with a real, live bank employee. The point has now been reached where it is possible to see a queue of people at an ATM outside a bank during opening hours while the cashiers inside are unoccupied. The speed of service has therefore declined (although since this is often due to the customer's own choice, this could be considered unimportant). More importantly, from a business viewpoint, the cashiers are now unable to 'sell' additional services to customers and this role has passed to the ATMs through the use of screen displays advertising additional services which are shown on the ATM while the transaction is in process. Has the service improved? Why do customers prefer to wait outside instead of approaching a cashier who has probably been through a customer care programme and can offer friendly and efficient service?

The perceptions of receivers and providers of the service are obviously different. The only way to discover those differences is to talk to the customers. At least with the present arrangement, customers do have a choice – and choice is a fundamental part of good service. In hotels, one of the service aspects found irritating is the lack of provision of tea- and coffee-making facilities in the rooms. Many hotels provide such facilities. A number of the 'better' ones – and certainly the more expensive – do not provide such facilities, assuming, presumably, that their customers prefer to use room service than to make their own beverages. However it would be nice to have the choice.

Talking to customers through some structured programme aimed at eliciting their views on a range of matters has another advantage. It enables the organisation, in addition to finding out the cause of complaints, to discover what it is about the current offerings that are liked and valued by customers. When providers of services talk to customers they often spend a disproportionate amount of the time trying to discover customer perceptions of bad or missing service. Questionnaires and interviews are often constructed in such a manner that forces customers to find negative things to say, even though their major perception may be of good service. If asked often enough, long enough and hard enough there are always negative attributes to a product or service that can be identified and discussed. This can be counterproductive – the customer who originally had a positive view of the organisation and its services has now been forced to address negative aspects. These may stick in the mind of the customer to the degree that the overall impression changes from positive to negative. This is similar to the kinds of student feedback generated by colleges at the end of a particular course. This too tends to concentrate on 'what went wrong' rather than on 'what went right'. However, no one is suggesting that we do not attempt to discover such negative views – only that we balance any data collection process to discover both sides of the customer perception. Such information allows the quality, customer care or productivity programme to set about: (a) eliminating or minimising the negative characteristics of goods and services; and (b) enhancing the positive factors; and to consider transferring them to other offerings within the product or service mix.

It is surprising how often what the service provider feels is important is considered relatively unimportant by the customers. For example, in the car-hire business, recent research has shown that it is the hiring process, rather than the car itself, which dictates the customer's perception of an effective service. See Case example 11.3.

The same is undoubtedly true of the new car purchase. Prices quoted in advertising and promotional leaflets often give an indication that a particular car can be obtained for a relatively modest price. Only on enquiring further does the prospective customer learn of the various additions. Even assuming that the advertised price includes car tax and VAT, there are often a number of extra costs such as delivery charges, number plates and road tax which can add several hundred pounds to the 'basic price'. Such additions are obligatory and should be included in the quoted price.

A good customer care programme will, in effect, turn the traditional pyramid organisation onto its head. Normally, policies and strategy are developed at the top

> **Case example 11.3**
>
> Europcar conducted research which showed that the public perception of car rental was that it was a complicated transaction. It was difficult to estimate the full cost of a rental since the advertised rates were kept low to attract customers but there were a number of additional costs to be borne – for mileage covered, for collision damage waiver, for insurance, for VAT, and so on. Those customers who knew something of such additional charges were deterred by their existence (and by the fact that their magnitude was often unknown in advance since they were not 'advertised'). Customers who were not aware of these charges got a nasty shock on their first rental, and were unlikely to repeat the process.
>
> Europcar has published new brochures which give the full and final price that the customer must pay.

of the pyramid by the senior management team and then the effects of this policy and strategy making filter through to the customer in the form of a product or service. Adopting a customer care approach makes the organisation concentrate on the frontline service (normally at the bottom of the pyramid) and work back through the customer chain, involving the internal customer–provider relationships, developing more effective means of providing and enhancing the various products or services in line with customer needs. The management and administrative functions of the organisation are seen as being in support of this fundamental customer-oriented product or service delivery.

Customer service concept

In some sectors, the concept of a 'customer' is fairly new. Hospitals, schools and local authorities in general have traditionally offered the services they are obliged to provide in the way they see as being appropriate (within legal or governmental guidelines). There is often no clear goal being sought; the effectiveness is measured simply by whether they provide the service within their allocated budget. The era of privatisation and competitive tendering has done little to change that, as yet. The aim now is to provide a service at a cost that wins a tender – and tenders are often allocated solely on the basis of price. The quality of the service is very much a secondary feature. However, the consumers of such services are getting better educated and more demanding. They are starting to demand 'good' service, and will extend this demand to the providers of many of the public sector services. There may be possibilities for multilevel services being provided at different charging rates – although with many of the funding mechanisms currently in place, this would be difficult to achieve. However, the growth of private education over the past 20 years is evidence of the fact that customers make quality judgements of such services as they do with consumer products. Such organisations will have to ensure that they know what they are trying to achieve and what their consumers expect of them.

They can then start to set targets and measure progress and effectiveness in a meaningful way. Without this clear direction and constancy of purpose, effectiveness cannot be determined and therefore is unlikely to be improved.

As an example, the establishment of local management of schools puts increased responsibility and authority onto head teachers. Heads now have to manage significant parts of the overall school budget. Thus, a head may be responsible for paying for such services as the cleaning of schools: at the same time, such services may have been 'privatised' or put out to tender, even though it may be a part of the local authority, such as a direct labour organisation, that wins and administers the tender. The relationship between the DLO and the school is now much more like the normal trading relationship between supplier and customer, and schools – via the heads – are more likely to expect a fast, efficient, good-value service than they once did. The transition from monopoly supplier to competitive supplier is difficult to achieve, since it requires a fundamental change of culture and attitude – to a concentration on, and a commitment to, customer service.

Similarly, those organisations that supply to other industrial or commercial organisations may not readily subscribe to the concept of customer service; the term seems to be reserved for individual, end customers. Yet such organisations must pay the same kind of attention to their customer needs. The solutions may, however, be different. These organisations, in the light of the Single European Market, may find that the number of, and location of, their customers changes – hopefully the number increases! Supplying a different range of services requires different service policies and possibly distribution networks. Customer needs may have to be satisfied by technological and logistical solutions. How do we ensure that our goods are available at a customer's determined schedule if that customer is in southern Spain and we are in the north of England?

Paying attention to customer service requires supplying organisations to:

- identify their customers;

- identify their needs;

- meet those needs;

and to keep such an analysis and approach continually up to date. The needs of the customer, and the customer's perceptions of the organisation and its products and/or services, will change over time. The organisation must identify those changes and change with them.

Keynotes
The customer is the only legitimate judge of service quality.

Dealing with complaints is important; but more important is the logging and monitoring of them to discover what aspects of the provided service or product cause complaints to be made, and the modification of the product or service design and delivery to avoid the repetition of such complaints.

The frontline service can only be improved and maintained if all the other service points, in the customer–supplier chain, are improved and maintained in support.

Talking to customers through some structured programme aimed at eliciting their views on a range of matters has the advantage that, in addition to finding out the cause of complaints, it enables the organisation to discover what it is about the current offerings that are liked and valued by customers.

It is surprising how often what the service provider feels is important is considered relatively unimportant by the customers.

Organisations must ensure that they know what they are trying to achieve and what their consumers expect of them. They can then start to set targets and measure progress and effectiveness in a meaningful way. Without this clear direction and constancy of purpose, effectiveness cannot be determined and therefore is unlikely to be improved.

The needs of the customer, and the customer's perceptions of the organisation and its products and/or services, will change over time. The organisation must identify those changes and change with them.

Discussion topics
List a number of organisations which you consider offer good service, then try to determine what it is that makes you think of their service as 'good'.

Repeat the exercise for organisations which you think offer poor service.

Discuss the steps that would have to be taken by an organisation in the second group to move into the first.

Reference
1 Horovitz, J. (1990) *How to win customers: Using customer service for a competitive edge*. London: Pitman.

12 The CREST factors

Much of the discussion so far has stressed the need for involvement of all parts of the organisation and all levels of staff within the productivity improvement programme. It is a truism to say that people are the most important resource of any organisation – they are certainly the most flexible. Translating a productivity improvement programme into a series of working procedures depends entirely on the way in which the many individuals within the organisation, at all levels, react to the programme and the concepts inherent in it. This is the biggest single factor, and perhaps the most difficult to achieve, in ensuring the success of any top-line productivity improvement programme.

In Chapter 7 we discussed the way in which organisations grow and commented on the way in which typical organisation structures mirror the structures that occur in military organisations. An alternative way of looking at this situation and in explaining the nature of organisations is to look at the general changes that have taken place in the nature of work following the industrial revolution. Before this revolution there was a general 'craft' structure in which most people who were outside the agricultural field worked within a role that offered them a significant degree of control over what they did and how they did it. They were each individually responsible for their own output. The industrial revolution, with its reliance on large organisations, lead to the start of specialisation and much greater interdependence on other individuals who each contributed part of a total process. Scientific management extended this specialisation and rationalisation to leave highly structured processes which led to highly structured organisations. The kinds of organisations that we are now capable of building are a compromise between the two extremes of organisation. We can now build an organisation that incorporates work groups with a degree of autonomy (similar to craft working) within a federal structure that resembles the typical hierarchical structure. Individuals within this structure are capable of regaining the responsibility and autonomy they once had and the organisation should benefit as a result. However, people within such a structure must be treated differently than if they were in the highly structured, bureaucratic organisation.

The key issues to be addressed are identified here as the 'CREST' factors and discussed below: any programme of productivity improvement – especially a top-line programme – which ignores these factors is doomed to failure. It is important to note that these factors are interlinked and interdependent to such a degree that they cannot be addressed individually but must be part of an overall, integrated effort. The factors are:

- C   Commitment and Communication

- R   Respect

- E   Enthusiasm

- S   Security and Support

- T   Training

Commitment

The word 'commitment' has already been extensively used – but not overused. Commitment starts at the top. However, commitment is much more than an expression of support. The managements of many organisations have expressed their commitment in the past to management by objectives (MbO), work study, job enrichment, and a whole host of other techniques and approaches, many of which achieved little or no success and many of which are now part of industrial and commercial history. Commitment does not, and should not, start with panic reaction to a specific problem but from a declared mission, with a reasoned evaluation of a current situation and an awareness of the opportunities that exist for positive change. Commitment is not simply an act of faith; it stems from the above reasoning and a knowledge that the opportunities identified, and the success of the mission, are dependent on participation and involvement from employees in all parts and at all levels of the organisation. The commitment at the top must be total, both in terms of level and extent. It must include the full senior management team of the organisation and each manager must be fully committed to any initiative or development programme. That does not mean that any idea or concept such as a Quality, Customer Service or Top-line Productivity Improvement Programme will always be enthusiastically welcomed by senior managers who will then automatically offer their commitment and drive it through the organisation. Senior managers are as subject to resistance to change and scepticism towards new ideas as anyone else. What it does mean is that there must be a period of time in which senior managers are allowed to discuss and debate such a concept, to have explanations and information offered by a relevant 'expert' (often an external consultant) and to grow towards the idea. It probably requires strong commitment from the champion or sponsor of the idea to undertake this development process and it does require that, at the end of such a process, real commitment should have been gained. Members of the management team must not simply 'show' this commitment; they must demonstrate it in all they do and say. Commitment is then subject to the law of gravity: it starts at the top, but naturally falls to lower levels. It can, however, be blocked. It must not be '*mis*-sed'. Commitment can be blocked by *mis*understanding, by *mis*apprehension, by *mis*representation and by *mis*takes. Such blockages are all too easy to create by those suffering from misunderstanding or misapprehension. One effective way to minimise potential blockages is to allow it to flow through well-designed and open communication channels. Ineffective communication can turn the flow into a trickle!

Communication

There have been so many books and papers written on effective communications that to repeat the basic principles seems almost unnecessary. Almost! It is such a crucial part of the implementation process that it is worth repeating the most fundamental of the factors again and again; but in turn they are only worth repeating if they are going to be acted upon!

The single most important principle brings the two 'C' CREST factors together: commitment and communication. Effective communication starts with a commitment to communicate. It is pointless to superimpose onto an organisation any communications processes or methodologies unless there is a basic desire to communicate. That itself arises from the commitment to the matter to be communicated; the two are inextricably linked. Commitment to communication can overcome poor communication channels and poor communication devices. It can, but it shouldn't need to! The desire to communicate should force an examination of the structures, channels, techniques and methods of communication that are, or could become, available. This examination should result in the establishment of appropriate devices to allow the communication to flow throughout the organisation, assuming the other principles are also followed. A strong productivity improvement programme may require some specific communications media to identify communications closely with the programme and to differentiate them from other communications on other matters. This is discussed further in Chapter 14 on establishing the framework for a top-line productivity improvement programme.

The second major factor to remember is that communication is a two-way process and, again, return signals can be ineffective unless there is the same commitment to receive as there is to send. This means that downward communication must be undertaken using channels and methods that allow and encourage feedback, and also that upward channels must be established. One way that two-way communication can be encouraged is through the use of team briefing sessions in which teams and their leaders get together on a regular basis to talk about issues relevant to their work.[1] This echoes the philosophy behind other group techniques, such as quality and productivity circles, and can be combined with them. Such circles form natural briefing groups either individually or in combination. If productivity circles are a part of the top-line productivity programme, mechanisms must be in place that force the discussions in those circles to be addressed further up the organisation.

Another important point is that information is only readily perceived and accepted when it both relates to the individual's or group's current interest and needs, and also is consistent with the views and attitudes the individual or group holds based on prior experience. (This is why people select a particular daily newspaper: to offer them information in a form that is consistent with their established way of thinking.)

Information which is relevant to current interest or need but not consistent with current views will be attended to but may be rejected as 'unsound'. Other information which satisfies neither criterion will have to be presented very forcefully if it is to be accepted. Forceful presentation is a combination of selecting the right medium, the right intensity of presentation and designating the right source. Information, for example, will be treated differently according to whether it comes from a superior, a status-confirmed individual, an employee representative or from another source. (Again, this is why new authors like to include a foreword by an eminent person: to lend their book authority and credibility.)

Accordingly, it may be necessary to change attitudes as part of the accompanying support for communication concerned with a new venture such as a top-line productivity improvement programme. This is best done not by hectoring or badgering people into submission, but by allowing them to participate in the process that formulates policies, views, procedures and so on, and by allowing them to listen to the reasoning underlying the formulation of end-statements. If the reasoning is sound, and it addresses both the needs of the organisation and the needs of the individuals or groups who are responsible for the success of the programme, it stands a good chance of being successful.

Respect

In Chapter 2, mention was made of the different attitudes that prevail in Western and Japanese (industrial and commercial organisation) cultures with respect to employees. In Japan, all employees are treated with a high degree of respect, as being potential supervisors/managers and as being capable of contributing to discussions both on their own work and that of the wider organisation. In the West, they are often treated merely as resources to which things are done, as part of the process, rather than as agents who can have significant influence on the nature of the process. Thus, Japanese quality circles involve the training of the Japanese workers in techniques and concepts that would often be judged 'too difficult' or 'inappropriate' for a Western workforce. This lack of respect also shows in the forms of communication used (often one-way instruction giving) and, as a result, gives rise to an equal lack of respect on behalf of employees for the management. Employees who are working in a 'federal, craft' structure, such as that provided by the introduction of autonomous work groups, can only realise the benefits to themselves and to the organisation if they are treated with the respect that they, their skills and the structure itself demands.

Introducing respect into relationships is not easy. It starts back with that basic commitment and an attitude that offers opportunities and allows time for both sides to earn respect from each other. Thus the management must offer opportunities for employees to communicate their views and feelings; they must understand (and respect!) the attitudes, beliefs and norms that form those views and feelings, deal with them accordingly and offer appropriate positive feedback. In turn, this approach of showing respect to employees will earn the managers the respect of those employees. Like communication, respect is a two-way process. See Case example 12.1.

Case example 12.1

When it was first suggested at Avis Europe, the car hire company, that as part of its customer satisfaction programme, employees offering frontline service on rental desks should have the authority to offer discounts, refunds, vouchers and so on to complaining or dissatisfied customers, the senior management were worried that the employees would 'give the store away'. They went ahead with the move, empowering employees without recourse to any hierarchical chain behind them, and the results have been impressive.

Customer perceptions of service quality, identified through sampling studies, have been raised significantly, and the costs of the 'giveaways' have been minor – especially if compared to the administrative and managerial costs previously incurred through a process of complaint escalation.

Respect also has another side: that of self-respect. Individuals within an organisation will perform with excellence only if they perceive their own worth to the organisation. Similarly, work groups must feel a sense of esteem for their group and its contribution to the organisation. This feeling of self-respect is naturally influenced by the degree of respect that individuals and groups feel that they receive from the organisation – in the form of their immediate supervisors and the management team in general. It is almost certainly not necessary to make great changes to what is done or how, in order to increase the self-respect of individuals or groups. Often it can be achieved simply by ensuring that managers and supervisors take the trouble to explain the wider picture when communicating. Thus an instruction to transfer from one job to another can increase the self-perceived worth of an individual if the reason given is that the new job is urgent or important. This is a very simple example, but it serves to illustrate the point that *what* is done matters, but *how* it is done matters equally.

Enthusiasm

Engendering enthusiasm among a workforce is the process of providing motivation. Motivation of employees is, like many of the other factors we have so far discussed, often treated as a 'plug in and go' factor. We expect to get a consultant in who will tell us in a few days how to motivate our workforce, or we treat it mechanistically by implementing payment by results schemes and expecting these to produce a motivated workforce.

We have already made reference to the tendency in the UK to look for panaceas, and we have mentioned that 'human relations' was once considered for the title – when items like job enrichment, job enlargement and so on were the fashionable concepts to discuss (but rarely to implement). Although the fashion has moved on, we seem to have learnt little from those discussions, as do those managers who are subjected to many of the human-relations theories that form part of their management training courses. There seems to be a 'macho management' ethos which regards human relations as being slightly 'cissy' or effeminate: real managers give orders. (Perhaps this is because so many of our organisational and management structures and procedures are built on a model derived from military institutions.) Motivation is a complex issue but a rereading of many of those human-relation theories may remind us that generally people work well if they have rewarding work to do and if they are treated with respect. Thus, the concentration on the 'humanisation' of work which is evident in the rest of Europe (and particularly in Scandinavia) is not necessarily there because it is 'the right thing to do' but because it affects the performance of those whose jobs are 'humanised' and offers real benefits to the organisation. It is an attempt to move from enforced motivation to self-motivation.

Establishment of a productivity improvement programme that is based around productivity teams or circles is itself a job-enriching factor which shows respect for employees' views and should produce an enthusiastic response from the workforce. Such a response is only likely to be forthcoming if there are no pre-existing industrial relations problems, and thus it is important to involve employee representatives in the discussions leading to the formation and establishment of the productivity programme to avoid the kinds of misunderstanding that can otherwise occur. Again such a communication and discussion if handled correctly demonstrates a respect for the employees and their representatives.

Security
In Chapter 9, when discussing the development of creativity and imagination, we referred to the fact that fear of failure is a strong negative motivating force. This is true of fear generally. Security is a basic human need and a workforce that feels insecure is unlikely to be at its most effective. Unfortunately there are times when a particular organisation, because of its financial position, may itself be in an insecure position. In such cases, on the part of the employees, another fear comes into play – the fear of not knowing. Almost certainly rumours and half-truths will abound. The only way to prevent such damaging informal and inaccurate communication is to respect (that word, again!) the employees and to explain the position to them. They won't like what they hear, but they will probably accept it if the underlying reasons are explained.

Support
Support takes a number of forms. There is the basic psychological support that arises from the respect of one's superiors and the freedom that accompanies this respect in being offered control of at least part of one's own activity, within agreed parameters.

There is also the physical support offered by the provision of appropriate facilities: tools, information sources, an effective working environment and so on. This can include support agencies to offer assistance in the use of specific techniques, specific hardware and so on. Without an acceptable level of support, appropriate to the task being carried out, energy is dissipated and motivation and morale will be eroded.

We are suggesting in our approach to productivity improvement that it is important that specialist productivity practitioners, whether internal or external, are seen as being there to support productivity teams and/or steering groups – offering training and guidance in the use of specific techniques, suggesting possible approaches, collecting data on behalf of such groups and generally responding to their requests for support and assistance.

Training

UK industry seems to have some form of aversion to training. Approximately 70 per cent of Britain's population leave school at the minimum leaving age; the same percentage (70) had only cursory training for the job they had when they started work; and the same percentage, yet again, have had no further training. That means that about a third of the workforce in the UK has had no training – ever! The reasons for this are not clear. Perhaps it is yet another legacy of the British class system under which people were, by birth, either destined for 'greatness' and thus needed no training or destined to be 'workhorses' and thus needed the absolute minimum of training required to carry out a specific, menial job. The concept of 'development' seems to have arrived late on the scene and to have been paid lip service only.

A review of the success of information technology implementations in the UK in 1989 showed that many organisations were less than happy about the perceived effectiveness of installed equipment. A clear reason stated for this was that many users had received little or no training and a large proportion of them had not even been supplied with the appropriate instruction manuals.

This habit of keeping employees 'in the dark' extends to the UK's commitment – or lack of it – to participation. Yet we have already seen that we are in an era of greater change than at any other time. We need a workforce that is able to adapt to the changing environment. Frederick Herzberg, when discussing retraining programmes for older workers, said that 'resurrection is much harder than giving birth'. What he meant was that if you leave employees to become out of date, the step to bring them up to date is too great for many of them. What is needed is a continual programme of development that constantly keeps them up to date or, better still, requires them to keep *themselves* up to date.

In the UK, it is generally assumed that shop-floor employees are either unwilling or unable to be involved in any form of development programme that does not offer direct and immediate financial reward. Yet it is just an assumption! There is little or no evidence to that effect. At one time, schemes such as job enrichment and job enlargement were seen as providing highly motivated, multiskilled employees. Such schemes were adopted on the whole in a meagre fashion with little real commitment either to the philosophy or to making them work. The concept fell out of favour and another great industrial panacea was thrown on the scrapheap. This lack of commitment to new (or even old) ideas crops up regularly in discussing the failures for one initiative or another. That is why this book stresses it above all else.

Training and development is not something to be 'bolted on' by the personnel department. It must be an integral part of the way in which the organisation itself operates.

The well-known demographic timebomb that is about to hit the UK, and much of Western Europe, in the next few years will leave organisations having to deal more carefully with the recruitment and retention of staff, in the light of increasing competition with each other for scarce human resources. Staff development programmes will be one way of tying employees to the organisation. Such programmes may also be used as the basis of providing opportunities for employees to learn more about the nature of the organisation, the inter-relationship of its constituent parts and the roles played by different individuals and groups. Such development offers opportunities for organisations to build programmes which provide employees more capable of taking part in the kind of discussion and debate, idea generation and critical evaluation that form the heart of a top-line productivity improvement programme (TPIP). Thus the demographic changes we see today as a threat may turn out to be beneficial in the longer term.

Training with regard to a TPIP includes two distinct types. One is the normal job-related training needed to ensure that employees work with the tools, equipment and other resources at their disposal in an effective manner. The second is training in productivity-related issues, including the nature of the particular productivity programme being implemented within the organisation. Such training is mentioned in Chapter 14.

Productivity improvement depends for its success on education and training. Similarly, quality control begins with education and ends with education.[2] Employees can only be expected to give of their best when they know what is expected of them – and, just as importantly, why!

Each of these CREST factors has been addressed very briefly; that is not because they are unimportant but because they are not the essential meat of this book. It is assumed that most readers will be aware (if only they could remember) of the factors and that the purpose of this chapter is to stress the importance of remaining aware during all planning and activity and in taking action which demonstrates that awareness.

Keynotes

Translating a productivity improvement programme into a series of working procedures depends entirely on the way in which the many individuals within the organisation, at all levels, react to the programme and the concepts inherent in it.

Members of the management team must not simply 'show' their commitment to the

TPIP; they must demonstrate it in all they do and say. Commitment is then subject to the law of gravity: it starts at the top, but naturally falls to lower levels.

Effective communication starts with a commitment to communicate.

Communication is a two-way process and return signals can be ineffective unless there is the same commitment to receive as there is to send.

Management must offer opportunities for employees to communicate their views and feelings; they must understand (and respect!) the attitudes, beliefs and norms that form those views and feelings, deal with them accordingly and offer appropriate (positive) feedback. In turn, this approach of showing respect to employees will earn the managers the respect of those employees. Like communication, respect is a two-way process.

The concentration on the 'humanisation' of work which is evident in the rest of Europe (and particularly in Scandinavia) is not necessarily there because it is 'the right thing to do' but because it affects the performance of those whose jobs are 'humanised' and offers real benefits to the organisation.

There is little or no evidence to support the assumption that shop-floor employees are either unwilling or unable to be involved in any form of development programme that does not offer direct and immediate financial reward.

Discussion topics
The rise of 'business and management studies' in the educational provision, the educated manager and theories of human relations has been paralleled by the decline in the performance of UK manufacturing industry. Is there a causal relationship?

The importance of commitment to productivity improvement, especially from the senior management team, has been continually stressed. How does this commitment arise? Can it be 'infused' into an unreceptive or unwilling workforce through motivational techniques or approaches?

References
1 Feldman, D. (1989) 'Team briefing', *Work Study*, Vol. 38 No. 10, pp. 12–15.
2 Ishikawa, K. (1985) *What is total quality control? The Japanese way.* Englewood Cliffs, NJ: Prentice-Hall.

PART FIVE

The top-line productivity improvement programme

Introduction

We should by now have discussed enough of the nature of productivity, and top-line productivity in particular, to realise that, although it is only an option available to an organisation, it is an option that increasingly turns into a necessity. The question becomes not 'Should we start a productivity improvement programme?' but 'How do we do so?' We have discussed sufficient of the underlying concepts and issues to turn now to a programme for achieving higher productivity. This is the top-line productivity improvement programme (TPIP). As we move through this action programme, we will address additional and more practical issues, and in a more detailed way. We are still not able to provide a prescriptive programme of action; that depends far too much on the nature of a particular organisation, its environment and its ability to change. However, the framework we shall lay down should be sufficiently detailed for organisations to adapt it, with confidence, to their own circumstances. Some organisations may require the benefit of external assistance; others may be happy to proceed with the programme being devised and taken forward by their own personnel.

The fundamentals of the action programme are:

- establish the mission;

- assign responsibilities;

- establish the objectives;

- review the present situation;

- implement any structural changes;

- establish 'operational' processes and procedures;

- establish monitoring and control processes;

- identify staff training and development implications;

- DO IT!

Overall responsibility for the programme must rest with the senior management of the organisation as a team responsibility since the programme will have implications for all parts of the organisation. However, the actual detailed planning and control of the programme may be delegated to an individual who acts as the programme manager or co-ordinator. This individual must be a member of the senior management team in order to demonstrate the high-level commitment that is so important to the success of any such programme. Since the implementation of a top-line productivity action programme is a project-based activity (although the ongoing activity translates into operational activity) there must be a project plan for implementation and a project management system for overseeing the implementation. This is especially true because projects of this type which have a long life often suffer from two common afflictions that characterise many project-based activities. These are:

- *Background mode operation.* Many projects are started off with a blaze of publicity, with a high profile and with significant levels of activity. This initial burst of enthusiasm can be sustained for only a limited period and there is often a phase during which the project 'plods along' in the background and interest starts to wane. This is particularly true when the project is settling down and the detailed work has begun. There are, as yet, no appreciable results to be publicised to maintain interest and commitment. An effective project management approach ensures that the programme retains its impetus during such periods.

- *Finishing fatigue.* When a programme is nearing the end of its life (in this case when most of the parts of the programme are in place) there is a tendency for the final details to be handled with less enthusiasm since some of the people involved are already moving on to, or at least thinking of, another project. For example, when a new software package is created, one of the tasks carried out towards the end of the project is the preparation of user documentation. This is often rushed through to meet marketing deadlines and because many of those involved in the project are ready to move on. Yet, this documentation, as with the final details of many other projects, is crucial to the success of the overall project.

The management system may not be complex but it must exist. One way of achieving this, and of maintaining the communication to all involved parts of the organisation, is to establish a steering committee to receive regular progress reports and to discuss future activities and issues. Although committee structures have had a 'bad press', often being associated with lack of progress, they are useful as communications devices. If the responsibility for progress rests with the programme manager, it is possible to get the best of both worlds – effective managerial control and effective communication.

The rest of Part Five works through the stages identified above and offers guidance on the kinds of issue raised during implementation of this kind of programme.

13 Establishing the mission

Implementing a top-line productivity improvement programme (TPIP) is a radical venture for most organisations; it will affect the way the organisation is structured, the way it acts and, most importantly, the way it thinks. Changing the way in which the organisation (or more properly the individuals within it) thinks requires a strong and clear signal. That signal identifies the new direction for the organisation – the new mission.

The mission statement has become a fashionable asset for an organisation. That does not, of course, mean that it is invalid or unnecessary. It is important that all organisations are clear as to their basic purpose. An effective mission should create pride, enthusiasm and a will to succeed. For small and new organisations, the mission is usually obvious and generally unstated. For larger and diverse organisations, it may be less clear and it is then more important that a mission is identified and publicised. Managing a mission is a complex activity but the rewards from successful mission management are considerable.[1] The mission statement is a means of allowing staff to identify with the aims and aspirations of the organisation and should influence their role within the organisation. This is especially true when the mission changes.

A review of management systems and procedures of a number of successful companies[2] revealed a commonality which suggests that management is effective when the following factors apply:

1   There was a known corporate objective which was capable of being divided into smaller elements, thereby providing a number of specific objectives for the various departments within the organisation.

2   In all instances there appeared some form of structured communication which was specifically aimed at both encouraging and assisting information flow up, down and across the organisation.

3   Regular performance reviews on a corporate/departmental/divisional basis.

Thus, the success factors start with an identification of the corporate mission. The aim of producing a mission statement is to:

1   Make a statement of the basic purpose of the organisation.

2   Set a framework which can influence policy making and target-setting.

3   Avoid suboptimisation of objectives at lower levels of the organisation.

4   Signal to all interested parties (customers, employees, suppliers, shareholders, community charge payers, etc.) the basic aims, philosophy and values of the organisation.

5   Attempt to influence/change the organisation culture.

Since the mission statement is to be widely publicised and aims to influence a range of interested parties, it may be necessary to include statements directed specifically at each of these interested parties. It should be written in a brief form but one which leaves those reading it in no doubt as to what the organisation is attempting to do and to achieve; it should also be written in such a way as to enthuse those reading it and to make them want to play their part in achieving the mission. It most definitely should not be a vague 'For God, Queen and Country' type statement offering all things to all readers, tagged onto the organisation since all its competitors have one.

Creation or revision of the mission statement is an ideal time to incorporate the aims of, and values inherent in, a TPIP. Conversely, implementation of such a programme is an ideal time to publicise a (new) mission statement.

The mission statement is the first stage at which the commitment to top-line productivity improvement is demonstrated. It must therefore draw attention to the changed values inherent in a TPIP and it must be followed, reasonably closely, with other publications, communications and, especially, actions designed to enhance that commitment.

The mission statement is obviously the responsibility of the senior management team of the organisation; but it should result from consultation and discussion with a cross-section of organisational membership and even with interested parties from outside of the organisation. The first stage is to ask simple questions such as:

● Who are we?

● Why do we exist?

● What is our fundamental purpose?/What business are we in?

● How do we wish to be perceived by others?

● What distinguishes us from our competitors?

● What is our customer/client community?

● What is our supplier/service community?

● What dictates our environment?

● Which groups do we need to influence?

For many organisations, answers to some of these questions may be influenced by a constitution, articles of association, legal charter or other document.

The questions should be answered wherever possible in a number of stages, moving from the general to the more detailed. For example, an organisation that runs long-distance coaches should identify itself as being primarily in the transport business, then in the road transport business and finally in the coach travel business. This process should identify the core values of the organisation,[3] values which should shape the objective setting and strategy formulation processes.

Having attempted answers to these questions – perhaps in a series of workshops or seminars – one should try to determine long-range objectives for the organisation and to prioritise and group or classify these objectives according to the part of the organisation or its environment to which they principally refer. This identification of objectives clarifies the mission and it may need an iterative process moving from mission to objectives and back to reconsideration of the mission. The connection between the mission statement and the major long-term objectives must be made. If major objectives are not seen to be reflected in the mission statement (and preferably derived from it), the mission statement requires revision. Similarly, it is necessary to identify major constraints on the organisation's activities and to ensure that the mission statement is consistent with these.

Once a draft mission statement has been prepared, it is essential that it is widely discussed to ensure that a consensus emerges. Where a mission is significantly different from an existing situation (and an implied existing mission), this must involve effective communication as to the need to change the mission and the ways in which the new mission is to be implemented.

After these discussions, and possible redrafting of the mission, an attempt should be made to edit down the mission statement. What can be left out without detracting from identification of the basic purpose and attitudes of the organisation? The briefer the statement of mission, generally the clearer the mission becomes.

Once a mission statement has been formally drawn up, issued and publicised there may be a demand for substatements. Mission statements can be used at subunit levels of the organisation but they must be seen as being directly supportive of the organisational statement and they must naturally be subject to the same kinds of constraint as the organisational statement – especially with regard to being firm and positive rather than vague and 'woolly'. Additionally, in a large multifaceted, organisation, it is necessary to ensure that subunits are not duplicating specific sub-missions.

The acid test of a mission statement is whether it influences and drives the corporate planning process. If planning can be carried out and objectives set, both short term and especially long term, without reference to the mission statement, then the mission is not fulfilling its purpose. The mission may include aspects which could be considered 'secondary' in terms of fundamental purpose. For example, a profit-making organisation may include within its mission statement entries on service to and support of the local community. It is vital that such entries are not there solely for public relations purposes with no commitment to ensuring their involvement in the planning and control cycle. If so, their public relations value becomes at best minimal, and, at worst, negative.

A mission statement does need monitoring and review, but it should serve to stand for a significant period of time (at least two or three years) since it is, in effect and in part, a summary of long-term aims and aspirations. After this time period it should be possible to review the mission and to establish that organisational planning and activity resulted from and contributed to the declared mission.

Of course a mission is not created or amended simply to serve the interests of a TPIP. If anything, it should be the other way round. However, the thought and development processes that lead to consideration of issues such as productivity, quality, customer service and value-for-money – all component parts of a top-line programme – may lead to or stem from the consideration of mission. The senior management team may, naturally, consider missions which have nothing to do with productivity (although in the way in which we have redefined it, that would be very difficult) or may have other mechanisms and policies for delivering a chosen mission. For example, it is common nowadays for organisations, especially larger ones, to undergo a process of corporate identity review. The (re-)establishment of a corporate identity is an image-building process, but also has internal effects in terms of creating a particular culture and in improving employee morale by making them aware of the nature of the organisation that employs them and values them. Establishing a new corporate identity can be an expensive business. It involves perhaps a consultancy exercise – and corporate identity consultancy is expensive – redesign of company buildings, logos, liveries, uniforms, stationery and so on. These costs are an additional burden on the operating parts of the company and thus can be said to reduce productivity, since the outputs remain the same while the inputs (the resources consumed) rise. However, if we continue to look at top-line productivity as being the sum of factors that add value to products, there could be a claim that an effective corporate identity does in fact add value, and thus increase the top line of the ratio.

It is well known that many organisations buy IBM computers for reasons other than the inherent technical quality of the machines: the overall image presented by the company is one of solidity and stability and there is a common quote that 'no one ever got fired through buying IBM'. The job of the senior management team is to consider the ways in which the mission can be delivered, and to prioritise activity in a number of areas. It is important to ensure that where a number of avenues are explored and utilised, the activity in each one is complementary to and supportive of other activities. Thus a corporate identity programme can sit easily alongside a top-line productivity programme – if they both stem from a clear organisational mission. In fact, a corporate identity review generally considers the same kinds of basic questions that must be answered when undertaking a mission review; the two are dependent on a fundamental assessment of what the organisation is and where it is going. The corporate identity programme is one route to ensure that it gets there.

Where a mission is being reviewed or created as part of the implementation of a TPIP, it is essential that the major top-line factors to be addressed within the programme stem from the mission. Thus if quality is a major factor to be addressed, the mission should make clear and concise statements about the attitude to quality. Quality, especially at mission-setting levels, tends to be misinterpreted. It is often assumed to mean 'goodness' and used in very vague ways, such as: 'We intend to offer the highest quality of service ...'. Quality is concerned with conformance to agreed standards of manufacture or levels of service and especially to customer perceptions of value. Those standards, levels and perceptions will be determined with respect to the target market and with regard to financial constraints. Thus a commitment to high quality means knowing the standards you, and your customers or clients, set and adhering to them. Quality thus applies at all levels of the market: companies targeting low-price, volume markets can offer high-quality goods – it simply means that their agreed standards are adhered to. In the motor industry, for example, quality does not mean fitting leather upholstery and walnut dashboards, but that the plastic dashboard – if that is the standard set – should be properly fitting and functioning. Thus the aim of the mission is to define the 'contract' in broad terms between supplier (the organisation) and customer and then between the organisation and the workforce, the organisation and suppliers, etc.

The mission statement should then be used to determine effective structures, systems, policies and plans based around the concept of the TPIP. The key ingredients for a change or reidentification of mission are:

- recognition of the need for change;

- a clear vision of the future, shared by key agencies and individuals;

- a system for bringing about that vision;

- immediate actions in support of the new mission.

Where an organisation creates a new mission in an attempt to change the way it operates and is perceived by its customers, it must ensure that it is capable of being seen as credible in the minds of its public. An attempt to include statements on quality or customer service within a mission is laudable; but it is dangerous to go public with such a mission statement before ensuring that the organisation can 'deliver the goods'. A number of public utilities, in preparation for privatisation, came out with declared missions, new logos, slogans, etc.: British Telecom – 'It's you we answer to', and British Rail – 'We're getting there', are two obvious examples. Such organisations were, however, perceived as the 'old' public sector organisations with the same set of values, culture and practices. The mission is instantly devalued in such a case and the customer perception of the organisation may actually be reduced. The public (the customers) rightly question the amount of money being spent on publicity and image-building when their perceptions of the basic product or service make them feel that this is where the investment is needed. Contrary to what some advertising people seem to think, Abraham Lincoln was right when he said: 'You can not fool all the people all of the time.'

We have already stated that a mission should be published and publicised as soon as possible after being established; this publicity should, however, remain internal to the organisation until the culture and operation of the organisation is sufficiently in tune with the declared mission to be recognisable by the customers and clients.

Too many organisations spend time writing a mission statement and then file it away and get on with 'the real work'. The importance of the mission defining or driving the establishment of corporate goals cannot be overstressed. Obviously, if the goals are to be real and practicable, there must also be some system for measuring progress towards and achievement of such goals. That is why the strategy and planning process which succeeds the establishment of the mission is all part of the same continuum.

A mission must become a vision. That is the job for the senior management team – not as managers, but as leaders. Leadership and management go hand in hand, but they are not the same thing. Later, we shall be suggesting ways in which structures and procedures can be established to implement a TPIP. That programme will only achieve major success if it is led, and recognised as being led, from the top. The process of establishing such a programme through a declared mission will require changes to the organisation, to the tasks it performs and, especially, to the way it performs them. These changes must be part of the total vision which established the mission.

In the case of an organisation that includes productivity, quality or customer service within the mission statement, there is a commitment to providing a strategy, a planning process and a monitoring and control process that ensures that the values in the mission statement translate into clear and measurable aims and objectives and a plan for implementation of procedures that serve to reach them. That is the purpose of a top-line productivity improvement programme.

Keynotes
The mission statement is a means of allowing staff to identify with the aims and aspirations of the organisation and should influence their role within the organisation.

Success factors start with an identification of the corporate mission.

The mission statement is the first stage at which the commitment to top-line productivity improvement is demonstrated.

The mission statement is the responsibility of the senior management team of the organisation but it should result from consultation and discussion with a cross-section of organisational membership and even with interested parties from outside of the organisation.

The identification of objectives clarifies the mission and it may need an iterative process moving from mission to objectives and back to reconsideration of the mission.

Mission statements can be used at subunit levels of the organisation, but they must be seen as being directly supportive of the organisational statement.

The acid test of a mission statement is whether it influences and drives the corporate planning process.

Discussion topics

Examine one or two published mission statements of organisations with which you have dealt and evaluate the degree to which the mission can be identified from the customers' or clients' perspective.

Write a draft mission statement for an organisation with which you are familiar. Give it to someone else and ask that person to identify the organisation (or at least its field of activity).

References

1   Campbell, A., Devine, M. and Young, D. (1990) *A sense of mission*. London: Hutchinson.

2   Blacker, G. (1987) 'Performance management in the Royal Borough of Windsor and Maidenhead', *Management Services*, Vol. 31 No. 3, pp. 12–16.

3   Linkow, P. (1989) 'Is your culture ready for total quality?', *Quality Progress*, Nov. 1989, pp. 69–71.

14 Creating the framework

A top-line productivity improvement (TPIP) programme arises from the organisational mission; it must be part of the overall organisational culture and drive. It is not a bolt-on technique superimposed onto an ineffective organisation to change it into an effective one; and the programme cannot thrive in a hostile or unsupportive environment. Neither can it be regarded as a programme that is independent of the rest of the organisational strategy: it therefore requires to be included in the full strategic planning process of the organisation and seen to be contributing to high-level corporate aims and objectives. This statement is important. It means that management cannot rely on such a programme to do their work for them: the productivity improvement programme is part of the organisation's strategy; it is not the complete strategy. Additionally, there is no point in making a commitment to such a programme without ensuring that the prerequisites and the 'delivery mechanisms' for implementation of any strategy are firmly established. Thus, before the programme is implemented we must provide a framework that allows the programme to perform its purpose. The programme should not be introduced, in an operating sense, until the organisation is prepared for it. Once a clear mission has been established, there must be structures and mechanisms which translate this mission into policy and activity.

There have been various suggestions as to the methodology of implementing productivity improvement programmes. One such example arises from the work of the United States General Accounting Office, which identifies seven key elements in an effective productivity management effort.[1] These key elements are:

1   a manager who serves as a focal point for productivity;

2   top-level management support and commitment;

3   written productivity objectives and goals, and an organisation-wide productivity plan that establishes priorities for these goals and outlines actions needed to meet them;

4   productivity measures that are meaningful to the organisation;

5   a measurement system to hold managers accountable to the productivity plan;

6 awareness of productivity's importance throughout the organisation and involvement of employees in the productivity effort;

7 an ongoing activity regularly to identify productivity problems and opportunities
   for productivity throughout the organisation.

These seven points echo much of what we have been discussing within this book, but
they represent very much a management-led approach. The involvement of
employees is included within the key points, but what we need is a framework and
an implementation plan that ensures that such involvement is not only addressed but
is central to the programme.

The framework necessary to support a TPIP consists of the organisational
structures, the organisational systems and the responsibility and reporting procedures for the programme itself. Any attempt to introduce a TPIP, especially on a
phased basis, must be based on 'vertical slicing' of the organisation.[2] Those involved
in the programme may represent only part of the breadth of the organisation but
must represent a slice through the whole depth. Shared involvement with and ownership of the programme is vital. This can be taken to including common training of
people from these vertical slices.

Traditionally, training is operated on a horizontal-slice basis in that those being
trained are all at the same hierarchical level. The importance of establishing full
vertical commitment and commonality of purpose may make vertical-slice training
for productivity improvement a preferred alternative.

The organisation structure – and possible changes – in terms of creating an
organisation that has a high potential for change associated with productivity review
and improvement has been covered in Chapter 7, but this chapter makes additional
points specific to the organisation of the productivity improvement programme
itself. These points must be carried through in the structural planning, carried out
with regard to the principles outlined in Chapters 7 and 8. The full benefits that will
accrue to the organisation will only come from a combination of addressing the
organisational issues and providing the structured programme of productivity improvement. As before, the changes and procedures described in this chapter are not
intended to be prescriptive but to offer a model that can be used, and/or adapted, by
an organisation as the basis for establishing their own programme. This may sound
like a 'cop-out' but there is no panacea; each organisation is different in its existing
form, is operating in a different environment and has a different potential. These
differences must be recognised in the design of the productivity improvement
programme.

The organisation structure adopted, at both the macro and micro levels, is
designed to offer a potential for effective working; but that potential is only realised
when the structure is completed by 'cladding' it with the procedures that link
together the various parts of the structure into a working whole. This collection of
procedures is the operational 'system' of the organisation (more accurately, a set of

operational systems) that transforms the raw materials and other resources into the final product or service. As with organisation structures, operational systems tend to grow in an ad hoc manner as the organisation grows, with very few being systematically reviewed or designed.

In some organisations, and especially larger ones, there may be a review of parts of the system as part of formal work study, systems analysis, organisation and methods (O&M) or business review processes. Irrespective of any such formal reviews, the system often receives additional 'kick-starts' or other shocks with such events as the introduction of new products, new processes, new technology, new scales of operation, and so on. The system thus undergoes some modification when it must be adjusted to cope with such changes. Such changes can, however, be dangerous: they are often made on a 'needs-must' basis with little regard to longer-term, structural or system issues. The introduction of a top-line productivity improvement programme is such an event that requires the system to be reviewed and amended. Since the programme may be accompanied by organisational change, it is even more important that the system is reviewed and redesigned. More importantly, the occasion offers opportunity for a complete (or holistic) system review. It is not suggested that this should be a once-and-for-all review that must be carried out before a productivity improvement programme can be implemented, but rather that the structures and procedures set up for the programme themselves become the mechanism for a wider review. The full review of the workings of the organisation thus becomes a part of, but not necessarily a prerequisite for, the productivity improvement programme.

Nor is this chapter suggesting that a TPIP cannot be implemented without a total reconstruction of the organisation. However, the review and restructuring process does enable the maximum potential for benefit to be obtained. It has been suggested that organisational restructuring can be a threatening process for employees of the organisation. This is especially true of the managers of the organisation who have their cosy 'empires' well delineated. However, review of structures should not be avoided simply because it may upset this present, comfortable arrangement. If the senior management team is 'afraid' of this change process, their commitment to the total absorption of a productivity review process must be in doubt.

One of the problems with the book as a medium for presenting information is that it is essentially a linear, serial access device: readers start with Chapter 1 and work their way through to the end. This chapter, for example, follows from those on organisational review and design. The structure and the systems are so inextricably linked that in practice changes to them will not be carried out serially but in parallel, with each influencing the other. That is why this chapter refers to the framework – a framework in which structure, systems and procedures are inextricably linked.

Structures and systems tend to be hierarchical: there is a grand overarching structure and system which can be seen to be made up of a number of smaller substructures and subsystems. Thus it is important to review, and to confirm or modify, the overall structure and system before attempting to change the details involved in these subsystems. In this case (establishing a TPIP), this must be done to include the programme within the activity of the organisation.

Each system is itself made up of a number of components, principally technology (where technology includes such basic things as buildings and office furniture) and people. Since the organisation structure essentially covers the ways in which the people interact, it becomes clearer that the system must complement the structure. It is, for example, inappropriate to define a structure that includes working groups or teams which are physically distant – unless technology can provide the effective communication mechanisms needed for group working. If the structure represents the bricks that make up the organisation, the system is the mortar that binds the bricks together. The chapter on organisation structure identified the importance of information flows as determinants of effective structures – this is naturally true of systems as well. The system consists of:

- the buildings;

- the furniture;

- the process technology;

- the operational procedures;

- the information/communication provision;

- the managerial and control procedures;

- the clerical and administrative procedures;

- the supporting services;

and the people. A system can only be successfully introduced when the people are prepared for it. This may simply mean that the people must be prepared by having the new system carefully and completely explained to them, or it may mean that significant training and development work needs to be undertaken (especially where a new system involves a radical change of technology).

As we have stated, the introduction of a TPIP does not necessitate a complete review of all organisational systems, but it is likely that some, at least, will need to be reviewed and amended. (Those organisations that fail to attack productivity improvement because they are waiting for a convenient time to undertake such a review may wait for ever.) Similarly it is not necessary to *change* all the system components but it is essential to *review* them all and to ensure that all necessary changes are made and that problem areas, for example buildings that are unsuitable and cause problems of 'organisational distance' where people who should ideally be brought together, cannot be, are identified and either 'solved' – by using technology to ensure effective communication between different sites – or incorporated into some forward planning process. When this happens it is important to recognise those changes which have 'knock-on' effects on other systems. The degree to which system changes are necessary will probably depend on the extent of organisational and cultural change that has been determined necessary to support an effective programme of top-line productivity improvement. Changes in culture from a highly bureaucratic control process to one of devolved responsibility, for example, will lead to changes being necessary in administrative, and probably financial control, procedures. Some system changes will be necessary, in any case, to support a changed performance or productivity measurement and reporting regime.

The hierarchical nature of the systems means that some must be addressed as part of the structural review; others can be left until that review has been concluded and the new structure is established. This high-level system review must be a senior management responsibility.

The establishment of the productivity programme must then be accompanied by a low-level systems and procedure audit and review that will both establish those new systems necessary to support the programme, and review those changes consequentially necessary, or desirable, to existing systems and procedures. Since the changes are going to be across a number of areas of the organisation, this is probably best accomplished by a team of specialists (either in-house or from external consultants supporting the productivity programme) working with representatives of the operating areas and major central support functions involved.

This working team is vital to the success of the programme and should be set up as part of the overall restructuring process since it is an 'organisational' problem. The main purpose of the team is to initiate, direct, co-ordinate, monitor and review activity, progress and priorities. As the programme is to be central to the organisation's activity – and its future wellbeing – there should be a high-level programme officer or co-ordinator. (Co-ordinator is perhaps the more 'politically' acceptable title since it correctly stresses that major activity will take place within operational units rather than at the centre.) The productivity co-ordinator is the focal point for information and effort, the main point of contact for the specialist support teams and the clearing house for ideas. The appointment of the productivity co-ordinator (PC) is a major demonstration of action in support of productivity improvement, and the level of appointment (preferably reporting direct to the managing director or chief executive) is a measure of the importance assigned to the programme. In large organisations, the PC's role may be a full-time one; in smaller organisations it will, of necessity, be a part-time role. Where the role is part-time, it is important that the individual who is to fulfil the role of productivity co-ordinator does not have a major conflict of interest. The role may best be filled by someone from a staff or advisory position, rather than from the mainstream hierarchy. See Step 1.

The job of the PC is to establish the overall methodology for the productivity

---

Step 1

Appoint a high-level productivity co-ordinator.

---

improvement programme. This will include the establishment of a suitable measurement and reporting regime to ensure that the aim of improved productivity is actually realised. This methodology, but not necessarily all the measures, must be in place before the improvement programme is established – or even fully planned. The PC therefore needs some time, and probably some assistance, to discuss with the senior management the nature of the programme and to commence discussions on the type of measures which are appropriate. Discussions must also take place with line managers and with employee representatives, since there may be resistance to the changes being, or about to be, introduced arising from suspicion that this whole exercise is another way to 'police' or even usurp the line managers' role or to make the workforce 'work harder'.

Trade unions will normally react well to a programme that involves the active participation of their members in idea generating: where this is not the case, it is probably a symptom of underlying industrial relations problems which are pre-existent. Careful explanation of and discussion over the aims and nature of the exercise should serve to allay fears. It must be pointed out that a top-line productivity improvement programme adds responsibility to the roles of both managers and workers and that increased involvement with the organisation and increased job and role satisfaction should result. It may be difficult to 'sell' the concept of increased involvement and responsibility to a workforce accustomed to the normal way of doing things (where they are told exactly what to do and how to do it) without some corresponding financial reward. Whether financial incentive or reward for participation should be made depends on the organisation, its relationship with its workforce and naturally on its financial state. It should be possible to design and introduce an agreement which offers the workforce some share in future benefits arising from their participation and contribution to the scheme. However, direct financial reward for effort put into a productivity programme of this nature is usually inappropriate. The programme is a partnership venture and involves the whole organisation. Individuals or specific groups may be rewarded but not in cash terms. Financial rewards should arise from a long-term agreement for all parties to share in the future prosperity of the organisation.

The co-ordinator needs some knowledge of specialist areas which are likely to be incorporated within, or influence, the programme, and thus those with a productivity services background may be the most appropriate. However, detailed knowledge of such matters may be provided by specialist, in-house support staff or external consultants. It is just as important – if not more so – that the PC has a clear and comprehensive knowledge of the organisation and its business and is fully aware of the nature of the productivity mission and any structural changes needed to support it.

The PC must also evaluate the effects of the programme on other central services and central functions. In a previous chapter it was suggested that the role of central functions, such as quality, maintenance and engineering, may have to change if the new structures are based on a work group approach. Discussions must be held with representatives from these central functions to ensure that their role changes progressively as new structures and procedures are brought into existence.

There are a number of 'delicate' areas to be discussed and this means that the personal and communication skills of the PC are likely to be tested to the full.

The co-ordinator will also be responsible for the initial and primary communication media and messages. Should the organisation establish a news sheet to inform employees about the productivity programme and the results that emerge? If so, when should it be set up? Before the programme gets under way – so that it can be used as a vehicle for 'spreading the word'? Or at a later stage of the programme, when interesting stories and results are available for promulgation? Should the programme have a snappy title and its own logo? These are the kinds of questions that must be addressed. Such issues may seem trivial but we have already seen that communication is an important part of ensuring the effectiveness of the programme. It is useful if communications about the productivity programme are immediately identifiable as such – an eye catching banner and/or logo on messages can serve this purpose. Any name assigned to the programme should reflect the flavour of the programme within the particular organisation and may be dependent on the particular culture of the organisation. Some examples, offered purely for interest, are given in Table 14.1. They or their derivatives may be used freely!

Table 14.1 Possible programme titles

Programmes	Circles/teams	News sheets
A new DORN – DO it Right Now!	T3 Teams – Think, Talk, Try!	Team talking
Go4It!	Joint Action teams	
Profit through Productivity		The Productivity Connection
The Right Way		The WriteWay
PIP (Productivity Improvement through Participation)		
Top-line Programme	Top-line Teams	Top-line Trends

The Top-line Trophy can perhaps be awarded to the 'best' circle or team.

To ensure that the programme is seen as all-embracing, the name of the programme and any accompanying logo can be used to decorate and identify relevant documents such as information sheets, training materials, notepaper, prizes and awards.

Case example 14.1

The Productivity Co-ordinator is responsible for:

Advising on policy
Establishing the programme
Establishing the measurement regime
Establishing the reporting/information system
Establishing the structures
Creating training programmes

Training
Co-ordination/compilation/prioritisation of projects
Preparation of progress reports
Review

Data collection for measurement and reporting

Annual review and reporting

The appointment of the co-ordinator and most of the other actions listed in Case example 14.1 should take place before the official launch of the programme. That launch must be followed by some prompt action and for this to be done the major parts of the framework must be in place, and the conceptual planning should have been completed. The activities below can be carried out before or after the major launch, as they can be seen to be resulting activities demonstrating action in support of the initiative.

It is not possible for the PC to deal with the detail of each and every subphase of the programme – there is thus a need for the appointment of other staff. These may not be full-time appointments but there should be subsidiary officers or co-ordinators (or facilitators) in each of the operating divisions or units and in each of the major support areas (e.g. Finance, Personnel). These should be people who will, of necessity, make a significant contribution to the programme and may be line or staff employees in the units. Ultimate line responsibility rests with the managing director or chief executive and through that post to the major line managers, but certain responsibilities will be delegated to the productivity co-ordinator and the unit co-ordinators. The appointment of such co-ordinators also serves to demonstrate the organisation-wide influence of the productivity programme. See Step 2.

Step 2

Appoint co-ordinators in each of the major operating and support areas.

Unit co-ordinators may be best selected from the ranks of middle managers. These are the people who, we have suggested, may feel most threatened by the productivity programme, and the nature of a top-line approach. It is therefore useful to have their involvement. They should also already have some overview of different parts of the organisation. Naturally it is essential to select those members of middle management who have understanding of, are committed to and are enthusiastic about the concept of top-line productivity and the introduction of productivity circles (if these are to be a major plank on which the programme lies). Additionally, they must be effective communicators and 'sensitive' to the needs, aspirations and fears of others who are to become involved in the programme. The concept of quality circles outlined in Chapter 10 appears to offer an effective means of obtaining wide involvement in a TPIP and is used within this guide programme for this purpose. It is possible to use other mechanisms for achieving involvement, but unless such mechanisms are formally introduced as part of the overall programme, the wide 'ownership' that is necessary to utilise and motivate all staff fully is unlikely to be achieved.

Such co-ordinators may not all be appointed at the same time. A decision may be taken to implement the TPIP on a phased basis, with one or two areas being singled out to be used as pilot studies. Experience with these pilot areas can then be used to fine-tune the approach before extending the programme across the organisation.

Although it is sensible to undertake implementation on a pilot basis, there must be a clear signal at that time that the programme and the circles are to be extended to the rest of the organisation. If an attempt is made to restrict the approach to a specific part of the organisation, tensions will undoubtedly occur. The part of the organisation selected may think itself chosen because it is 'very good' or 'very bad' and others may view those involved as some kind of elite group. Those outside the area may cause problems that affect the area within the programme.

In order for the programme to move further it is important to provide some form of training to the unit co-ordinators to advise them of their role and responsibilities, of the support services available, and of possible approaches. See Step 3.

Step 3

Prepare and implement training plan for co-ordinators.

This training should be carried out by the central productivity co-ordinator in conjunction with support specialists (or external advisers). The training must include all phases of the programme from concept through to implementation and to review and evaluation. One way of describing these phases, and of providing a structure for the training programme, is to break the programme into a number of distinct subphases. One simplified description is shown in Figure 14.1. Each of the boxes in

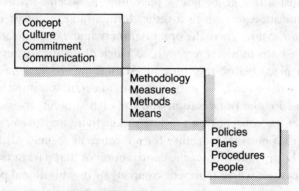

Figure 14.1 Top-line production training modules.

the figure represents one module of a possible training programme. The first module ensures that the overall concept of the programme is firmly established. It should also stress the importance of involvement of all people and the equal importance of keeping them informed of what is happening. Any communication devices established specifically to support the programme can be introduced here.

The second and third modules, although planned at this stage, will not be delivered until later. The second module starts to move towards the activities that must be undertaken to implement the programme. The productivity and performance regime – both in terms of its aims and the actual measures to be used – can be defined here. By the time that it is delivered – at least after Step 4 – those on the course should have some knowledge of this regime since they will have been involved in discussions that led to its formulation, but this may be the first time they have seen the 'definitive', finished product. The third module translates this implementation phase into specific plans, techniques that may be of assistance, and gives details of those who should be involved and ways in which this involvement can be assured.

Once co-ordinators are aware of the nature of the programme (in terms of the three boxes in Figure 14.1), the planning for developing the full programme should begin. The reason it is left until this – possibly late – stage is that it is important for these co-ordinators – on whom the success of the programme depends – to be involved in that planning process.

The establishment of appropriate top-line productivity measures has already been discussed. At this stage of the process the points made in that discussion must be addressed and the management team, with the help of the productivity co-ordinators and the specialist support staff, and in conjunction with those who are to

---

Step 4

Establish the measurement regime.

---

be measured, must arrive at a suitable measurement scheme involving a range of global and subunit measures which together form a range and pattern of measures which effectively measure where the organisation is at any one time and can be used on a comparative basis to measure progress. Much of the discussion on this matter will have taken place before this time in establishing the rationale for the programme; but now there has to be some attention to detail. It is important to identify the key measures for the organisation and for each subunit, to ensure that these adequately reflect the concept of a top-line productivity improvement programme, and that the various measures together form a coherent regime. Also, each subunit measure should be an indication of the contribution of that part of the organisation to the overall measures which represent company or organisational performance.

No attempt should be made to measure or evaluate the work of particular productivity circles or activities. A number of the benefits of circle working arise from the prevention of problems as much as the solving of existing ones. This would almost certainly not be reflected in the measurement and evaluation process. The measurement regime should thus measure performance of the organisation and significant sections of it: the success of circle activity will contribute to these measures.

Productivity measurement is almost as much an art as a science. There must be personnel available who are experienced in the concepts and practices of measurement and who are capable of communication with operating and support divisions since, once the measures have ben established in concept, they must be agreed with those responsible for achieving the results that contribute to the measures. It is important that measures taken in this part of the cycle are considered 'fair' by those subjected to them and that these people acknowledge their responsibility for achieving success in these designated areas. If the measures are agreed, perhaps after some discussion and even negotiation, appropriate data collection and reporting procedures must be established so that the measures can be compiled to an agreed time schedule. This is necessary in order to monitor the effectiveness of the programme. The measures themselves must arise from the objectives that have to be achieved. Once the measures and supporting procedures are in place, the planning of the productivity improvement programme can commence. This is part of the implementation process and is discussed in the next chapter.

The establishment of productivity co-ordinators in each unit does not mean that line management has abdicated its responsibility for productivity improvement. Groups should be established within – and even across – units to represent the line authority. These may be productivity steering committees or liaison groups and have two major roles. One is that they, like the circles which are shortly to be established, have a responsibility for raising ideas and suggestions and initiating particular studies and reviews. Secondly, they provide a forum to which ideas raised by productivity circles can be channelled for formal analysis and evaluation, for prioritisation and for the establishment of planned activity in furtherance of such ideas. These groups include those who have control of, or paths into resources that may be required to further particular ideas. Such steering committees may include one or more representatives from the productivity circles. There are basically two schools of thought on this matter. The first suggests that the steering committee may be less inhibited by the exclusion of circle representatives (but the inclusion of the unit co-ordinator ensures that ideas have a 'fair' hearing); the second that ideas, written down at circle meetings and reported back by unit co-ordinators, can be better 'sold' to the steering group by those with direct responsibility within the area concerned. See Step 5.

Step 5

Establish productivity steering committees.

The purpose of involving line managers in this way is not to control the people involved in the process, nor to control the ideas generated, but rather to ensure that the processes involved remain appropriate and that control is exercised on follow-up activity arising from the ideas generated by the circles. Without such a supporting control process there is a danger that ideas and suggestions are welcomed but not acted upon. In many ways the 'control' exercised is as much on the managers themselves, since the formation of the group and the resulting discussions at these meetings tend to ensure that those involved treat issues in a way that is consistent with the changed culture.

The frequency of meetings may depend on the confidence placed in the co-ordinators but is likely to start off by mirroring closely the scheduling of circle meetings themselves. In time, the meetings may become less frequent, with certain necessary functions delegated to one or more of the members; but since the group is itself, in effect, a productivity circle with a responsibility for generating ideas, there should be a minimum frequency of meetings established as part of the overall control process.

The framework is now established, and all members of the organisation should be aware of their degree of participation in the programme and the mechanisms for operating it. This framework lays down the bones of the system required to implement the productivity programme and this itself causes the wider system(s) to be reviewed and amended as part of the programme itself. Thus, the fuller review process of which we spoke earlier is addressed as part of, and not before, the productivity improvement programme.

Productivity ideas should be generated 'from the bottom up' by the productivity circles and 'from the top down' by the steering committees. Naturally a number of the ideas and suggestions will meet in the middle; there will be similar, duplicate and complementary ideas. The role of the co-ordinating officers is to ensure that advantage is taken of such commonality of viewpoint.

Once it is under way, there must be a process by which the programme is monitored and reviewed. This is in two stages. There will be regular reporting of results from the measurement programme and these can be used by productivity circles and steering groups to highlight possible problem (and success!) areas as the basis for future priority consideration. At the second stage, there must be review of the strategy for the improvement programme itself. This, again, is the responsibility of the senior management team. The PC, who should have sufficient seniority to be regarded as part of the senior team, will make regular reports on developments, progress and results. The programme will of course be reviewed as part of the standard strategic review process.

Our organisation (see Figure 14.2) is now starting to look 'messy' but this is a positive sign rather than a negative one. It shows that the boundaries and demarcation lines that we have associated with traditional, hierarchical structures are not being allowed to form.

Recognition

The issue of recognition was alluded to briefly in mention of awards or prizes. Recognition may take a number of forms. One is simply that those teams or circles who have produced what are felt to be particularly effective results can be allowed to make a presentation of their work to either or both of the main steering committee or representatives of their peers. This helps others to see the kinds of things that can be achieved and may start a competitive culture. An alternative is to present such results in the news sheet; but the sense of recognition is stronger with the face-to-face presentation. Further recognition can be provided by a trophy to be awarded to and held by the 'best' team for a given period (e.g. a month) or perhaps a banner or some kind of highly visible device to be erected at the place of work of the team. In the initial stages of the programme, it may be advisable to make some form of presentation to each circle as it raises and addresses its first major issue. Even before that stage is reached recognition can be given by registering each circle, with its chosen name, and producing a certificate of registration or plaque to be placed on the wall where the circle meetings are to be held.

Recognition to individuals, if it is felt necessary, can be afforded by presenting certificates following attendance at a given series or number of training sessions. Teams could be invited to special lunches or other functions or be presented with suitable small prizes. A particularly effective action or suggestion (e.g. a real blockbuster) should be rewarded in some special way.

178

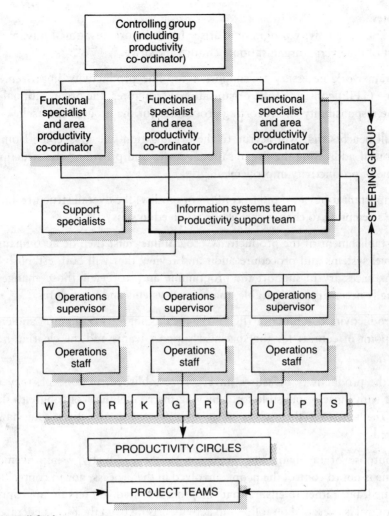

Figure 14.2 Full fluid structure.

The purpose of such recognition schemes is to offer (non-monetary) rewards which will maintain impetus to the programme and demonstrate the importance of the work done by the teams/circles. They also can be used to introduce a sense of 'fun' into the programme – to make it enjoyable as well as interesting and challenging.

Mechanisms are now in place to ensure that productivity is high on all agendas, with responsibilities assigned to key people across the organisation and procedures established to encourage ideas to be generated, analysed, discussed and furthered to give positive results. The organisation also has a means of measuring and evaluating these results. The programme can now start rolling!

Keynotes

A top-line productivity programme arises from the organisational mission; it must be part of the overall organisational culture and drive.

The framework necessary to support a top-line productivity improvement programme (TPIP) consists of the organisational structures, the organisational systems and the responsibility and reporting procedures for the programme itself.

The full benefits that will accrue to the organisation will only come from a combination of addressing the organisational issues and providing the structured programme of productivity improvement.

It is important to review (and to confirm or modify) the overall structure and system before attempting to change the details involved in subsystems.

The establishment of the productivity programme must then be accompanied by a low level systems and procedure audit and review that will both establish the new systems necessary to support the programme and to review those changes consequentially necessary, or desirable, to existing systems and procedures.

The productivity co-ordinator (PC) is the focal point for information and effort, the main point of contact for the specialist support teams and the clearing house for ideas.

Once the productivity measures have been established, in concept, they must be agreed with those responsible for achieving the results that contribute to the measures. The measures themselves must arise from the objectives that have to be achieved.

The purpose of involving line managers in the productivity improvement programme is not to control the people involved in the process, nor to control the ideas generated, but rather to ensure that the processes involved remain appropriate and that control is exercised on follow-up activity arising from the ideas generated by the productivity circles.

Once it is under way, there must be a process by which the productivity improvement programme is monitored and reviewed.

Discussion topics

What signs indicate that an organisation is not ready to implement a top-line productivity improvement programme?

The productivity programme, action plans and measurement regime must be carried through to 'delivery'. Within the structure outlined, who should be responsible for ensuring this happens?

Who, within your own organisation, could become the productivity co-ordinator (PC) or subunit co-ordinators?

References

1 *Increased use of productivity management can help control costs*, United States General Accounting Office publication GAO/AMD–84–11, 1973.

2 Klekamp, R. C. (1989) 'Commitment to quality is not enough', *SAM Advanced Management Journal*, Vol. 54 No. 1, pp. 13–16.

15 Implementation

By now – if you have been following the book properly! – you will know that we have the framework in place. The productivity co-ordinator (PC) is in post and subunit co-ordinators have been established in at least those areas ready to take part in the pilot implementations. Steering groups are also positioned to provide the 'squared circle' and ensure that issues raised are discussed at a forum that can take – or at least recommend – decisions.

Thus the main agencies for driving the top-line productivity programme are in place. These are:

- the senior management team;
- the productivity co-ordinator;
- subunit co-ordinators;
- steering groups;

with the productivity circles – perhaps the most important part of the framework – to be established shortly.

Initial training and overall programme planning have been carried out and the only part of the jigsaw to be completed is the establishment of the pilot productivity circles. All in good time.

The implementation process follows on smoothly from the establishment of the framework, thus the steps involved here are numbered consecutively from the steps involved in the previous chapter.

The first (Step 6) is to decide upon or confirm the areas for any pilot implementation. This could be done by identifying areas where maximum benefit is expected (perhaps because the problems are, or are perceived to be, greatest) or where early success is anticipated. Early success is important in establishing a degree of momentum for the programme that can be used as the basis of reports in the news sheet or other communication media, hopefully to enthuse those who come 'onstream' later in the programme. However, it is also necessary to select areas that represent some reasonable cross-section of the organisation. It is not appropriate, for example, to select only service functions or only frontline areas since the commitment to including all parts of the organisation must be demonstrated early on in the programme.

Step 6

Establish priority/pilot areas for implementation.

This prioritisation must be carried out by the senior management team in consultation with the PC and relevant steering group representatives. It should be obvious by now that commitment is required from those in line management positions in the selected areas, and this is another factor that can be used as the basis for selection of pilot areas. It may be that one or two particular line managers have expressed stronger interest in the concept of a top-line productivity improvement programme (TPIP), perhaps as a result of prior experience or a recent management course they have attended, or out of simple interest. Such interest, and – hopefully – enthusiasm, should be harnessed. Once the areas have been identified the detailed planning process can commence.

The PC is responsible for directing and co-ordinating the productivity programme planning process on behalf of the senior management team but individual units may approach certain issues in slightly different ways because of their precise structure, or because of the nature of the people within the unit. It is advisable to allow for such local differences of detailed approach; but to ensure that each unit does not end up with a different direction, thus distorting the overall mission, the PC should prepare a planning framework – in effect, a pro-forma plan – outlining at least the major areas to be considered, which the unit co-ordinators flesh out in discussion with the PC. See Step 7.

Step 7

Prepare productivity programme planning format.

This planning format may be highly prescriptive or flexible, depending on the nature of the organisation; an organisation with many different operating units, organised differently may require a more flexible approach. It is essential, however, that each of the resulting plans demonstrates a commitment to productivity improvement and appropriate mechanisms for ensuring that it takes place. See Step 8.

Step 8

Prepare unit productivity programme plans.

The completion of (pilot) unit plans within this planning framework is an extension of the training and development programme for the unit co-ordinators. These unit plans will include proposals for the creation of productivity circles where this is a part of the overall programme concept (perhaps on a pilot basis and according to the guidelines laid down centrally by the PC) and for employee training. The plans will include details on feedback mechanisms, reporting procedures, etc. and will demonstrate that the productivity measures determined can be supported by information derived at an operational level and the degree to which each is appropriate to the particular unit's activity. It is also important that these plans are developed in sufficient detail to permit easy implementation; they should go down to the level of identifying frequencies of circle/steering group meetings, locations for those meetings, and so on. Specific resources required to support circle activity may also be identified. As a simple example, each circle may need somewhere to store documentation and papers associated with their meetings.

It may at this stage also be possible to identify systems or procedures which require immediate review. There is a danger in pre-empting the initial discussions of the circles themselves, in particular because the co-ordinator has identified areas of potential immediate or high payback, or for similar reasons unit co-ordinators attempt to 'make their name'. If the circles feel they are being manipulated in terms of having issues imposed upon them, they will lose ownership of their circle and the associated commitment. Therefore, circle time must be seen to belong to the circle members and, although the co-ordinators and leaders may make suggestions, the real discussion must centre on issues and problems raised by the circle members themselves. It is important that management do not use circle meetings as a convenient time when a group of staff are together to address their own issues or communication requirements.

The approach to productivity improvement is, however, a combination of top-down and bottom-up approaches. Thus, as part of establishing the unit productivity plan, the PC and the subunit co-ordinator must engage in discussions with the line management and supervisors within the unit. These discussions will centre on the wider issues. For example, many of the issues raised at circle meetings will refer to detailed aspects of the job, based at individual workstations and work areas. It is unlikely, though possible, especially later when the circles are active and becoming increasingly confident, that circles will introduce issues which relate to the whole (or sub-) process of providing a product or service. Such broader considerations of change must come from those who are responsible for the top-down approach. These issues should be continually addressed, even before the TPIP has been established, as part of the normal managerial process. The programme does offer a vehicle for ensuring that such issues are more formally addressed within a wider framework that co-ordinates and controls the development of such issues. The productivity plan is therefore an amalgam of a range of issues, some of which are addressed at the employee level (through the productivity circles), some of which are at the managerial level, and some of which are projects for specialist productivity staff.

It is the job of the productivity co-ordinator to identify knock-on consequences of addressing particular issues and to suggest joint or complementary activity. The unit co-ordinators, as part of this planning process, will also prepare a budget for their sphere of influence to cover such items as employee release to attend circle meetings. However, unless the services of central support and specialist staff are to be charged to units, these budgets will be relatively small. Demands for larger amounts of funding will arise from the activity of the programme but such demands will be subjected to some form of financial evaluation (such as cost/benefit analysis) as part of the development process. Nevertheless, it is important that some funding is released to the programme at a fairly early stage to demonstrate the commitment to the programme and to the furtherance of ideas raised. One way of achieving this is to allocate a small amount of seed money to each unit co-ordinator as a form of venture capital.

We are now nearing the stage where we establish the all-important productivity circles. Before this is done, it is vital that all those involved in the productivity framework are clear as to the purpose and operation of the circles. It is therefore wise to produce a guide, or a series of guidelines, to provide the circles with their 'operating environment'. This guide should emerge from the training and briefing programmes and discussions with and between the productivity co-ordinators and the unit co-ordinators.

Step 9

Produce guidelines for productivity circles.

Such guidelines will include information on:

- the purpose of the productivity programme;
- specific objectives to be achieved;
- the 'rules' for circle establishment and operation;
- the rights of and constraints upon circles and their members.

We are not at the point where the involvement of the workforce is requested. This can be done by holding a series of seminars in the pilot areas at which all employees in the particular area are present, so that in effect only those who will form one or two productivity circles are involved; or it can be done on a larger group basis. There is a trade-off between the cost of the sessions (in terms of the staff time involved) and the need to help the formulation of team spirit that can accompany small group sessions. One obvious consideration is that large group sessions may take too many people at the same time out of their main job function. Such seminars can be prefaced and supported by the production of handouts which employees can read at their own convenience and perhaps allow them, through prior consideration, to raise concerns at the seminars. A sample document is produced in Appendix A.

The concepts of, and reasons for, the programme are explained and the role and responsibilities of employees, both within and outside of any circle involvement, are communicated. This should be related to the role of any other bodies, such as steering groups, and to that of co-ordinators. It will also include dissemination of the guidelines for the circles. This may be a slow process involving discussion (remember, communication is a two-way process) and may be carried out by the productivity co-ordinators or by them in conjunction with any external support agency. These initial seminars must be followed by training sessions as detailed in the unit plans: the training should be handled by the unit co-ordinators, to establish their role, perhaps with help from support staff. This training is not a one-off exercise, however, to set employees 'off and running': the programme must extend into the future. See Step 10.

Step 10

Prepare and implement employee briefing/training programmes.

Since the basic concepts of the productivity improvement programme have been explained in the introductory seminars, these should not be repeated but reinforced. It is important to extend the employees' view of productivity to take into account the top-line factors and help them to understand the small part that increased rates of working from them actually have on overall productivity: the systems, procedures and methods adopted and used are much more important. Thus, their task is to assist in the development of improvements in these areas and not to 'work harder'. A schematic diagram, as in Figures 15.1 and 15.2, illustrating the concepts involved in top-line productivity is useful.

As the workforce becomes more confident in its ability to participate in the programme, the training can become more sophisticated. A number of the productivity techniques can gradually be introduced to the employees: certainly the basic charting techniques such as simple tree structure and cause and effect diagrams. The concepts of Pareto analysis and statistical quality and process control (perhaps under simpler names to avoid 'turning off' employees) can also be introduced along with basic data presentation techniques, such as histograms, pie charts and graphs, to enable employees to start their own data collection and recording procedures to provide data with which to extend their investigations and discussions. For example, employees should be given a basic approach to error analysis and identification, so that they become responsible for error detection and system change to effect remedies. The basic method study procedure (see Chapter 9) is a useful and simple

186

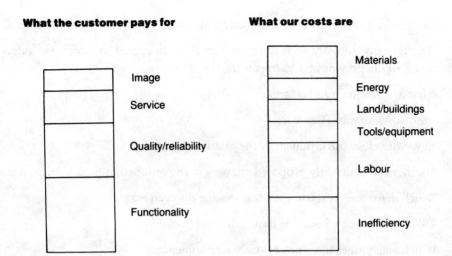

Figure 15.1

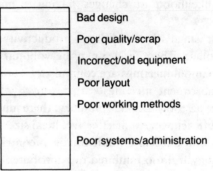

Figure 15.2

representation of an approach to tackling improvement – especially since they can now, through the productivity circles, become involved in all stages, and especially the SELECT stage.

Some of the techniques can be translated into checklists to aid the employees (along with such things as Pareto analysis and SPC) in decision making about areas to be tackled. For example, when looking at areas for investigation it is useful to record relevant background data, and making a simple checklist of questions can provide these base data.

1 What is the product?

2 How many units are produced annually/weekly?

3 What is the anticipated life of the product?

4 What are the stages in its production?

5   For how long has the current production process/method remained unchanged?

6   Are there any undesirable features (especially with regard to health and safety issues) of the present process/method?

7   What are the quality standards?

8   How is the quality assessed?

9   How often does the product fail the quality standards?

10   Are there any currently proposed changes in the production process/method?

11   Which departments/section are responsible for each stage?

12   Which stages does this circle have full control over?

13   Which stages does the work of this circle influence?

Questions such as these serve to illustrate the role that a productivity circle (and the work groups that the members of the circle come from) plays in the wider process and indicate the likelihood of changes having a major impact on improved productivity.

The important stage of establishing productivity circles now – or simultaneously – takes place. These circles may be voluntary or compulsory: it is recommended that the initial meetings are compulsory so that everyone finds out what is involved, but subsequent meetings can be on a voluntary basis. Naturally if attendance at circle meetings is to be voluntary, there must be enough volunteers for the circle to be of sufficient size to be effective. Ideal size is about 6 to 12 people; any fewer and the apparent 'burden' on individuals to contribute may be too great; any larger and people may feel too inhibited to contribute. In some sections or departments, voluntary attendance may result in the non-volunteers being unable to continue with their normal work since this is based on a critical team-mass: in such situations it is necessary to provide some other activity for those who do not wish to contribute to circle activity. Ideally, this should be something which helps increased productivity – either directly or indirectly – so that all employees remain involved in the productivity improvement programme. It may be possible to give some form of staff training, perhaps by holding training sessions or providing an 'open learning' facility that individuals can use on a personal basis; or, in some circumstances, such employees may be able to contribute to some cleaning or (preventative) maintenance programme. There is a slight danger that the alternative offered may be seen as being preferable to the circle activity and dilute the attendance at circle sessions but, if handled carefully, this should not be a major problem.

Where employees elect not to join a circle, there should be no pressure from either management or colleagues to change that decision. Alternative provision for non-participants must therefore not be regarded as a punishment or as in any way demeaning. Such employees are still 'part of' the circle, if not actually members and may be invited to attend specific meetings where a particularly relevant issue is being discussed or may be invited to submit agenda items or suggestions outside of the main circle activity.

Step 11

Establish productivity circles in the pilot areas.

It is essential that a circle leader is established. This, as we have discussed earlier, is normally a frontline supervisor from the area concerned but on occasion, where the supervisor is unable or unwilling to take on the role, it may be a selected or elected representative of the circle membership. A leader is required because at times the circle members may:

- be dominated by one or two aggressive individuals;
- select issues which are difficult to solve or resolve;
- have difficulties getting to meetings because of other priorities;
- feel management is being too slow in adopting and addressing its ideas and suggestions;
- get 'tired' and need some fresh impetus.

The leader must be trained to identify and address these issues and thus another part of the training package needed to support the introduction of the programme is training for circle leaders (Step 12).

Step 12

Establish and implement training programme for circle leaders.

The first meeting of the newly formed circles should take place a relatively short time after the circles are established. This meeting is almost bound to repeat some of the ground covered in the early seminar/training programmes but it is essential to make progress by ensuring that some 'live' issues are raised and discussed. A separate short briefing meeting between the productivity co-ordinator for the area and the circle leader to prepare 'prompts' that will allow circle members to raise such live issues may be required. The circle training sessions (which may involve employees from a number of potential circles – although this becomes less desirable as the need to engender team identity and spirit within each circle becomes paramount) will, in the search for higher top-line productivity, move from the conceptual description of the role of productivity circles to discuss the kinds of technique that may be appropriate either for use by the circles themselves or on their behalf by support staff. When it comes to the initial 'real' circle meetings, naturally restricted to the leader, possibly the subunit co-ordinator, and the members of that circle, some team-building and group dynamics exercises will be needed to help the circle start to form into a cohesive unit. These can include creative thinking exercises to encourage simultaneous thinking about the particular work area.

Circles are not committees and should not be troubled by the 'baggage' of the formal committee. They should thus not have formal agendas or keep formal minutes of their meetings. Reporting of what occurs, and more importantly of what must be done as a result, takes place through the structures that have been established and needs no additional tier of activity.

Step 13

Hold introductory circle meetings.

Mention was made in the previous chapter of the importance of clearly identifying the programme through the use of a particular name and/or logo to be used on all communications. This 'identification' can be taken to the stage of assigning names to individual circles – it is more appropriate to let the circles create their own name. This allows snappier reporting in the news sheet of progress made by individual circles. It is much more interesting to read that 'The Wire-Room Wizards have just ...' or the 'Finance Flyers propose that ...' rather than 'Circle No. 46 have requested that ...'.

These initial circle meetings will probably start by addressing the moans and groans of the workforce – moans and groans that no one has listened to before. This should not be discouraged; such complaints indicate a level of dissatisfaction, and that dissatisfaction itself has been gnawing away for some time at morale and efficiency. It may be that many of the complaints can be handled simply by the circle themselves, now that they have the chance to talk openly about them in a constructive manner; others will be passed up the chain by the circle leader and discussed in some other forum.

One useful analysis is to define each issue, problem or suggestion as controllable by the circle, partially controllable by the circle or non-controllable by the circle. Those that are controllable should be the basis of an action plan determined by the circle members themselves. Others must, in part at least, be communicated 'along the line' to steering groups through circle leaders and co-ordinators for further study or action.

A similar classification could be into issues which are actionable by the circle, actionable by the circle if given sufficient resources, or non-actionable.

Where issues or problems must be communicated upwards, it may be helpful to have a form or document to record the basic data about the issues: the circle raising it, the date, why it was raised, possible ideas for improvement and so on. This ensures that items brought from circle meetings to steering group meetings are done so in a consistent manner which should enable the steering group to consider them more effectively. The form must be introduced as a helpful, supporting document rather than as any way of monitoring what goes on within the circles. Some items may be passed to steering groups, some to an appropriate line manager, depending on the nature of the item. There should be a guaranteed response time for each item. For items passed to steering groups, this will have to be within x days of the next steering group meeting; for items passed to line managers there may be a fixed response time of, say, 48 hours. The response may not offer a full answer to the issue raised but should indicate what action is being taken and when, approximately, the issue should be finally resolved. Even where issues are not prioritised or not considered suitable for progressing, the group that raised the issue is likely to feel more content with a speedy, even if negative, response.

Some of the simpler measures must be implemented quickly, which is why some funding must be released to accompany the establishment of the programme. Where further study is required, the unit co-ordinators should request assistance from productivity support specialists on behalf of their circles, with reports on progress being carried back to subsequent meetings. This is why the introductory circle meetings must be followed quickly by meetings of the steering groups who will discuss the issues raised at the circle meetings and add issues/questions of their own.

Step 14

Hold introductory steering group meetings.

Again, some of the suggestions that arise from these introductory meetings will no doubt be very simple and capable of immediate implementation; others will require further study or investigation.

It is important that an action plan is prepared by the unit co-ordinator on behalf of the circle following the discussions by the relevant steering group and agreement with the productivity co-ordinator to establish areas of conflict/overlap. These action plans will be specific to the particular circle and are 'owned' by the circle: they will list the issues raised and identify what action is proposed to address each of the issues. They will thus include planned progress on both circle-controllable and non-controllable issues.

It may be that some issues are left in abeyance so that progress can be made on priority issues. Such priority issues must be identified by the circle but information fed back from the steering group via the co-ordinator may inform this prioritisation process. The first action plan cannot therefore be finalised until, at least, the second meeting when the first report back from the relevant steering group has been made. The action plan will make recommendations and assign responsibilities for action by the circle members themselves, for investigation and action by support staff (to be agreed by the leader of the support staff after co-ordinating the various actions required from all participating circles), by line managers (agreed at the steering group meeting or taken as the result of an issue passed directly to the line manager), or by the co-ordinator (usually information-gathering and administrative matters). It is important that the plan assigns responsibilities together with a schedule of activity and that a suitable progress record is determined and kept so that the reporting back of progress – for occasionally reasons for lack of it – to circle members and to steering groups is effective.

Step 15

Draw up productivity action plans.

These action plans then are used by the subunit co-ordinator to update the unit productivity programme plan. It may be that some of the suggestions raised by circles do not appear immediately to the steering group as being directly constructive in terms of improving productivity. However, a part of the action programme (and available resources) should be set aside to cater for what appear to be employee 'whims' since these will contribute to improved morale and indirectly to improved productivity.

Following this first phase of activity, there are bound to be areas of disquiet, areas requiring clarification and additional points of organisation or procedure raised. There should again be a quickly arranged meeting of the co-ordination team to discuss such issues and report back via the main co-ordinator to the senior management team.

Step 16

Hold review meeting of co-ordinators.

This apparent haste in holding the various circle, steering group and co-ordinator meetings is necessary to ensure that the procedure of the programme is understood, implemented and modified in the light of experience. Astute readers will realise the (time) resources that are being put into the programme and the reason why the commitment of senior management has been constantly stressed. It is likely to be some little time before the real benefits of the programme are realised, and the management team must be prepared for this investment in future success.

Once the action plans have been established and the review meeting has clarified any procedural points, progress must be communicated to all those involved. This may be done via the news sheet, via meetings, or in any other appropriate manner.

Step 17

Communicate progress.

The news sheet is obviously a one-way communication device and thus meetings may be necessary to obtain feedback. This can be achieved at subsequent circle and steering group meetings, which avoids the establishment of a separate forum for such feedback and ensures that communication is tailored to the concerns and aspirations of the circle themselves. Any other forum would serve to confuse and to detract from the importance of the productivity circle as the main driving force behind the programme.

At some stage, experience gained so far will be incorporated into modifications to the programme and to the organisation of new circles and steering groups as the programme moves from the pilot to full-scale implementation. Where implementation is being carried out on a phased basis, with only pilot circles being involved initially, a schedule for extending the programme into the other areas naturally has to be established. This should be done as quickly as possible to avoid the established circles being regarded by others as some sort of elite group – but after any teething problems have been overcome. This stage may be reached after two or three circle/steering group meeting cycles and after any minor changes resulting from the first co-ordinators' review meeting have been made.

It is important not to introduce new circles until the time is right. The PC must be satisfied that individuals in the area are fully aware of the concepts of the programme and the role of the circles and that a circle leader has been selected and trained. As the programme starts to move through the organisation, there should – hopefully – be a demand for more circles in areas not yet covered. The train is moving and everyone wants to get on board!

With time, as the circles and steering groups develop into their new role they will become more 'sophisticated' in their discussions and their requirements. For example, the circles will start to discuss issues that require more investigation. It has been suggested that this can be carried out by the specialist support staff. However, where an organisation has a large number of circles, the burden may become too great and the time schedule for such investigations may cause frustration among circle members. This should have been addressed when the employee training programme was designed. At the appropriate time (decided by the circle leader in conjunction with the local PC) the members themselves should be trained in certain data collection concepts and procedures. See Case example 15.1.

Case example 15.1

If a circle is discussing the amount of scrap or wastage produced, it may require an analysis of scrap produced and the reasons for it. One way of providing this information is to construct a simple tally chart so that each time an article is rejected by the quality control procedure, a tally is entered on the chart against the appropriate column and/or row entry. Circle members can be taught about data presentation methods, such as the use of histograms and pie-charts and can analyse the information they have themselves recorded as the basis of discussion at a subsequent meeting to determine priorities for further action.

Training is thus not a one-off exercise but a continual programme, tailored to the developing needs of the circles and their members.

Assuming all goes well, the programme should establish its own momentum. It may, however, require further inputs to maintain the original enthusiasm. This could be via additional seminars and workshops, by 'special events', by special news sheet issues, or whatever is deemed appropriate. One thing that may happen is that the circles start off with great enthusiasm and offer a range of suggestions that, because of resource constraints, take time to be included within the action programmes. Subsequent circle meetings may therefore continually address the same problems, with circle members becoming frustrated. There is an opportunity to 'fill' these meetings with additional training sessions – on productivity related matters such as charting and other recording techniques, time management, workplace layout, quality assurance, statistical quality control techniques, sampling methods, problem-solving techniques, health and safety issues, etc. Alternatively, where appropriate, the circle leader and co-ordinator may identify a theme for a future circle meeting – such as waste, energy conservation, maintenance or whatever. Together such proposals should lead to a circle membership more capable of taking responsibility for their own project investigation and action and therefore a more effective programme. In conjunction with specialist support staff and any training section the co-ordinating team must plan the introduction of such sessions and be ready to implement them at the appropriate time. It is not necessary for all circles, or even all members of any circle to be offered the same training. The training policy should be to respond to any needs identified by the circles themselves, and reported via the co-ordinator, and to supplement this response by offering the standard range of training packages devised to either full circles, to subsets of a circle or to training groups made up of representatives from a number of circles. Circles may identify training requirements which are work-based as a means of improving the productivity of the working group: again there must be a mechanism for providing such identified needs. Such a training policy or programme is likely to be much more effective if it responds to needs identified by the employees than if it is imposed by the training section because 'it is good for the employees'.

The main source of momentum is perceived progress and success, and this is only achieved if all involved treat the programme with absolute respect and commitment. Senior management must ensure this respect by their own continuing commitment and involvement.

At relevant intervals, specified when the measurement regime was established, there will be additional inputs to the programme from the results of the measurement and evaluation process. This should serve as a measure of success (though it is unwise to expect too much too soon) and a motivating factor. Where results are not encouraging, perhaps because changes made have not yet filtered through into the measurement process, or even occasionally because changes may be initially counter-productive but obviously have longer-term benefits, it is important not only that the management team maintain faith with the programme but that these results are interpreted by the co-ordinators so that circle and steering group members are aware of actual, as distinct from measured, progress and that some indication of the time span before measured results will demonstrate progress is given. Thus, one of the jobs of the co-ordination team is to make such predictions. These predictions should actually have been made when each activity or project was added to the action plan (as part of the cost/benefit analysis), so should not impose a great additional burden.

The 'tiredness' of circles referred to above should be, in part, matched by the need for circles to move from an initiation phase to a monitoring phase. Many of the improvements made will require positive monitoring and action to ensure that they retain their effectiveness. The results of measurement should be absorbed into the monitoring process and the circle will increasingly need to involve itself in this monitoring and control work. Thus the fact that the number of new suggestions may tail off is not in itself a major problem. However, it is important that the circles continue to raise new ideas and suggestions and that co-ordinators and circle leaders ensure that the increase in monitoring activity does not usurp all the time of the circle meetings and that space is provided for further progress.

Although this makes the establishment and implementation of a programme sound remarkably simple, it is not so. The above merely serves as a guide; any individual programme must be tailored to the needs and shape of the particular organisation. Although there will undoubtedly be problems and confusions, the will to succeed should surmount all such obstacles and provide success: without that will, the programme will fail.

What is important is that the implementation of the programme should follow a predefined plan based on the structure and framework that has been established.

Keynotes

The main agencies for driving the top-line productivity programme are the senior management team, the productivity co-ordinator, the subunit co-ordinators, the steering groups, and the productivity circles (perhaps the most important part of the framework).

Pilot implementation can be carried out in areas where maximum benefit is expected (perhaps because the problems are or are perceived to be greatest) or where early success is anticipated.

It is important that some funding is released to the programme at a fairly early stage to demonstrate the commitment to the programme and to the furtherance of ideas raised.

As the workforce becomes more confident in its ability to participate in the programme, the training can become more sophisticated.

It is important that an action plan is prepared by the unit co-ordinator on behalf of the circle following the discussions by the relevant steering group and agreement with the productivity co-ordinator to establish areas of conflict/overlap. These action plans will be specific to the particular circle and are 'owned' by the circle.

Training is not a one-off exercise but a continual programme, tailored to the developing needs of the circles and their members.

Although there will undoubtedly be problems and confusions, the will to succeed should surmount all such obstacles and provide success: without that will, the programme will fail.

Discussion topics

If an attempt were made to introduce productivity circles into your organisation, would there be a positive or negative reaction from employees and their representatives (such as trade unions)? If negative, how would you change this to a positive reaction?

Some employees may see the time devoted to circle meetings as either a waste of time or an opportunity to escape from the workplace. Who is responsible for counteracting these views and how can it be achieved?

16 Monitoring and review of the programme

This is one of the shorter chapters in this book – but by no means unimportant. A top-line productivity improvement programme (TPIP) is concerned with continual improvement; that philosophy must be extended to the programme itself. Monitoring and review of the programme, its methodology, the people involved, its structure, its processes, its communication media, its training programmes and its operation must parallel the monitoring and review of the results obtained. It is not possible for the programme to be implemented without problems. Any programme which is as far-reaching as a TPIP should be is bound to raise issues of conflict and of overlap with other activities. Since members of the organisation in all areas and at all levels are involved in the programme, they must also be involved in its monitoring and review. The establishment of a formal review procedure is the responsibility of the productivity co-ordinator (PC), but issues concerned with the operation of the programme, especially those of conflict and overlap, are bound to be raised at circle, steering group and co-ordinators' meetings. Thus the review is itself likely to be continual with a degree of fine-tuning going on all the time. However, there should also be at the very least an annual review of the programme to ensure that it is performing its function. It is difficult to lay down an exact process for this formal review since it depends on the exact nature of the culture that has been created, the management style adopted and so on. It may be that the PCs each conduct a review session in their own area of influence – through the circles and steering groups or using separate meetings involving representatives of circles and steering groups. The review must not be held in secret. All those with something to contribute should feel that they have the opportunity to do so; the programme is jointly owned by all members of the organisation and they must all be party to any review process and resulting changes.

The programme should not be condemned on the basis of early results: we have already indicated that a TPIP is a long-term commitment to improving productivity. It takes some time for productivity circles to 'find their feet': most employees have been kept in the dark and told to keep quiet for such a long time that asking them to contribute to such a programme may raise initial suspicions that take at least a few months – and some positive feedback – to dispel. Short-term results (up to six months) can be negative as the changes made to implement the programme may incur costs before they start to reap benefits, and measured results may take a short-term downward trend. This is one of the reasons why the need for the commitment of the senior management team has continually been stressed. This commitment must be sufficient to maintain the programme through any initial negative phase. Medium-term results, say after 12 months, should start to show beneficial changes, and trends which will indicate longer-term success. If our organisation is monitoring and reviewing its performance, both within and outside of the TPIP, then we can safely assume that there is an ongoing cycle of strategic, tactical and operational planning. The review of the programme must feed into this strategy formulation and planning cycle.

In the first year, the changes made to the programme should be of detail rather than of concept: changes may be required to particular parts of the structure or to specific procedures, but the basic methodology of the programme should be left unaltered until it is clear that either it has failed to live up to its promise (when we should ask the reasons why) or that there are aspects which are causing sufficient dissatisfaction to require change.

Where dissatisfaction exists, it should be first confirmed that the structures and procedures that were created to run the programme are still being adhered to. All practices and procedures are subject to drift. Sometimes that drift is positive: incremental beneficial changes are made to jobs and activities that are not recorded in job descriptions or work specifications, but are minor amendments made as a result of informal review or response to changing environments and situations. These positive changes are to be welcomed and should not give rise to dissatisfaction. Such incremental changes can also be negative. Well-defined and disciplined procedures may become ill-defined or sloppy: this can happen as those involved are under stress owing to high workloads or simply as a result of the nature of the individuals themselves. It is often a sign that the procedures were not specified in sufficient detail or were not wholly appropriate. Too detailed a specification can, on the other hand, lead to a bureaucratic and inflexible organisation with little room for individual initiative. There is a balance to be struck here. There is concern that such changes to jobs and activities may indicate a lack of real commitment to productivity and quality – which can be a sign that the motivation and driving force behind the whole programme is running out of steam. It is more worrying if the dissatisfaction felt has not been reported and discussed at a circle or steering group meeting, since this is one of the purposes of the meetings: to allow people to raise any matter with which they are unhappy. It is important to identify such signs early and to set in train a process of correction. This process, like the rest of the programme, should involve those concerned, by allowing them to express their dissatisfaction and by asking them to make suggestions for the remedial action. Unfortunately, as with quality itself, it is much more expensive and much less effective to impose quality control to identify errors than it is to ensure that things are performed correctly the first time.

Naturally, the outputs from the measurement regime, as the programme moves into subsequent years, should indicate that the results of the programme are satisfactory. However, as with the operation of the organisation itself, this does not mean that matters cannot be improved. What is required is a systematic review of the programme – in the same way that we expect the programme to provide a systematic review of operations. It must be recognised that the structures and procedures we have put in place to ensure the smooth running of the programme are now part of the status quo and changes to them may be resisted. If the programme itself is working effectively, this resistance should be minimal since change (lots of minor changes and a few major ones) should be taking place across the organisation as a result of discussions, ideas and suggestions raised within the programme.

Where external consultants have been employed to assist in the setting up of the programme, they may be used to conduct an impartial review; in effect, an audit of the programme. This impartiality can be useful since all those in the organisation have some degree of vested interest in the current operation of the programme. However, having set up a structure and procedures that are designed to generate change, it may seem like a vote of no confidence if outsiders are brought in to make the changes to the programme itself. This obviously needs careful handling by the consultants – and the process they use to undertake the review must involve those involved in the programme and recognise their interests. Where the programme has been established without outside help, the PC may require the help of internal support specialists in the review process. Anonymous questionnaires on the programme may be used as the basis of a basic data collecting exercise, but these will require to be supplemented by views obtained from the formal structure of the programme itself – from circles and steering groups.

When discussing the use of questionnaires earlier, it was suggested that there is a danger in looking only for negative feedback. Although there may be aspects of the programme which result in negative feedback, these are best shown up in comparison with those aspects which are regarded favourably. Any questionnaire must be designed to elicit both positive and negative responses. Any suggestions that emerge as to ways in which the programme may be improved or extended should be discussed at each forum and, hopefully, some consensus will emerge on a number of the issues.

Care should be taken before undertaking a major change in the methodology of the programme – such as deciding that productivity circles are not working or are too expensive and should be discontinued. Where such views are held it is essential to carry out an investigation that moves from symptoms to causes before decisions of such magnitude are taken. Certainly anything that diminishes the involvement of any one group in the programme should be treated with suspicion: that is not to say that changes should not be made, but rather that if one change were to cause such a diminishing of involvement, then an alternative mechanism should be put in place to ensure that the involvement continues.

Deming talks about establishing 'constancy of purpose'.[1] The review of the productivity programme must maintain and enhance, not interfere with, this constancy. Changes should only be made to the programme when it is not seen to be contributing to results that contribute to objectives that contribute to the mission; or when a way is identified to improve this contribution. As with productivity itself, the review is not only concerned with solving perceived problems but in taking advantage of perceived opportunities.

Keynotes
A top-line productivity improvement programme (TPIP) is concerned with continual improvement; that philosophy must be extended to the programme itself.

All those with something to contribute must feel that they have the opportunity to do so: the programme is jointly owned by all members of the organisation and they must all be party to any review process and resulting changes.

Early changes made to the programme should be of detail rather than of concept: changes may be required to particular parts of the structure or to specific procedures, but the basic methodology of the programme should be left unaltered until it is clear that either it has failed to live up to its promise (when we should ask the reasons why) or that there are aspects which are causing sufficient dissatisfaction to require change.

If any one change were to cause such a diminishing of involvement in the programme from any one group, an alternative mechanism must be put in place to ensure that the involvement continues.

Discussion topics
Most people enjoy the development work associated with a new project or programme; few relish the monitoring and control aspects of a project cycle. How does an organisation ensure that a programme, once established, is continually monitored and updated?

Impartial review of such a far-reaching programme can only be done by those with 'no axe to grind'. It is therefore essential to use external consultants to carry out a review of a top-line productivity programme.

Reference
Walton, M. (1989) *The Deming management method*. London: Mercury Business Books.

Appendix A
Introductory handout for employees

The nature and content of the handout will naturally be determined by the nature, title and style of the productivity programme to be implemented. This sample is offered as a guide only.

Why productivity circles?
The organisation is committed to improving our performance in all areas of our activity. That is why we have issued a new Mission Statement. This Mission Statement is not simply a few paragraphs to please our shareholders; it is a signal that we aim to improve what we do and how we do it, in all ways that we can. To do this, we need your help. Together we can look at everything that we do and suggest ways in which things might be improved. Productivity circles are the means by which we can get your help.

What are productivity circles?
Productivity circles are groups of employees who get together to look at problems or situations and make recommendations for change. These changes may be major or minor; they may be concerned with what you do or how you do it; with the tools, equipment, methods of work or the conditions at your workplace. Productivity circles will meet at regular intervals to discuss any item which the employees wish to raise. We will provide you with the time and somewhere to hold these meetings; what you discuss is up to you.

Who will be involved?
Hopefully, everybody! Attendance at circle meetings is voluntary but circles work best if everyone attends and contributes. You may decide to attend some meetings and miss others; it's entirely up to you. You will be invited to join a circle with other people from your work area so that you can discuss common problems and issues.

Who is in charge?
Each circle has a circle leader. The leader is responsible for organising the meetings and reporting back to management on the discussion and ideas that you have. This leader will be trained in productivity circle techniques and will train you in some of these techniques as part of the activity of the circles.

What's in it for me?

We are all part of the same organisation. We can only be successful if we all work together. This gives you a chance to say what you think should be done to improve your work. If the programme works, we all stand to gain from the company being more successful.

When do I start?

You will be invited to a meeting to explain things more clearly. You will then be invited to join a productivity circle. As part of the programme you will be given some training in productivity matters. If you feel that you need more help or training in a particular area, let your circle leader know. If you feel that the programme itself can be improved, this too can be raised at one of your meetings.

How long will it last?

The programme is a continual programme to make sure that we are always looking at ways of improving what we do. You can choose to be involved or not at any time.

Appendix B

The Top-line Productivity Improvement Programme

Establish the mission
(Commit the organisation to
continual productivity improvement)

Translate the mission into long-term aims and objectives

Carry out strategic planning

Review organisation structures

Appoint a productivity co-ordinator

Establish the methodology

Start spreading the message   Appoint and train subunit
and the methodology   productivity co-ordinators

Establish the measurement regime

Establish productivity steering committees

Select pilot areas for implementation

Prepare productivity planning format

Prepare unit productivity plans

Produce guidelines for productivity circles

Brief and train employees

Establish productivity circles and circle leaders

Train circle leaders

Hold introductory circle meetings

Hold introductory steering group meetings

Draw up productivity action plans

Hold review meeting of co-ordinators

Communicate progress

Extend the implementation

Monitor and review

Index